# A Historic Tour Guide

**Ron Freeman**

The cover illustration depicts the Sergeant Jasper Monument in Madison Square.

ISBN 0-9661521-0-7
Library of Congress Catalog Number: 97-77333

Published by:
H. Ronald Freeman
607 Washington Ave
Savannah, Georgia 31405

Printed in Tallahassee, Florida
by Rose Printing Company

# Acknowledgments

No one writes a book alone. There are many involved in such a project even though only one is credited as the author.

Many people gave of their time and counsel. Others offered the use of materials that could not have been obtained elsewhere. Everyone was busy, but all were gracious with their time and attention.

I would be remiss if I didn't mention Dr. John Duncan and the assistance he rendered in proofing the manuscript, separating fact from fiction as I strived for historic accuracy. Additionly, he was most generous in locating illustrations that had proved difficult to find. He is truly a resource when researching Savannah's history.

Lastly, I would like to thank my wife Judy, who was my editor and grammarian. She spent endless hours of rearranging and restructuring the formless mass of words I had thrown together. On occasion, I vetoed her corrections, so any remaining errors are mine.

# Preface

Savannah is a city bursting with true stories of her past just waiting to be told. Unfortunately, many of the details have long been lost or twisted in the retelling. Hopefully, through the research offered here, many of the missing facts will again be available to visitors and citizens alike. What I've attempted to provide is a factual handbook containing the background surrounding the historic attractions in the city today.

The book has been organized from a visitor's perspective, with the information arranged in a way that would satisfy my curiosity if I were touring a strange city for the first time. The facts and stories presented are drawn from published sources. Where there was conflicting evidence from creditable sources, I opted for the source that had the greater credence, unless sufficient documentation was available otherwise.

Savannah is filled with monuments and markers to the heroes and figures that once strode these streets. Who were they and why were these monuments erected? What was happening in the world they lived in and how did they alter those events - or flow with them? Lastly, what happened to these people after they left the spotlight? Where do they rest today?

In order to understand and appreciate Savannah, you need to go back to the beginning and come forward. Learn why the streets and squares carry certain names. Learn the intent of the founders and what they were trying to accomplish. By so doing, you will follow the characters that have strutted on Savannah's stage for over 260 years with all their tempers, passions, and foibles.

By knowing where Savannah came from, you can appreciate where it is today and what it has to show you. You also can understand that although the town is filled with stories and history, it is not a museum. The city is very alive and very conscious of its heritage. Best of all, Savannah's people are as interesting and charming as always.

Ron Freeman

## Table of Contents

# History

## Early Period

*Early Georgia inhabitants*

Most of us think of Georgia's beginning with Oglethorpe's landing in 1733. But even then, the land was populated by the Yamacraw Indians. In fact, thousands of years before the coming of the Europeans, Indian tribes populated the area. Evidence of this is apparent from the huge piles of ancient oyster shells known as "shell middens" left from the feasts of long ago tribes. Theirs was basically an agricultural economy. Judging by the pipe remnants discovered, we know one of the earliest crops was tobacco. The staple crop was probably corn.

By the time Europeans began exploring this region, the Indian population was in a decline. Early Spanish accounts of the 1500's describe the Savannah River basin as being practically uninhabited and a buffer zone between warring tribes to the north and south.

English colonies were already as far south as the Jamestown settlement in Virginia by 1607. From there they continued to push southward and in 1629 King Charles I of England claimed the Carolinas as English soil. This led to the settlement at Charles Town (it became Charleston after the Revolution) in 1670 and Beaufort in 1711. These settlements served to open the area southward for further colonization.

## The Colony

For some time the English Parliament had discussed forming another colony. A committee had been formed to study the ways a new colony could alleviate problems in England and create opportunities at the same time. Thousands of men were out of work, and when a man couldn't pay his bills, he was sent to prison. Soon the prisons were overflowing. The committee members thought a new colony would provide an ideal outlet for those who had fallen prey to the debtors' prison. As it turned out, almost all the colonists were extremely poor but only about a third of the original colonists were debtors. None had a history of being in a debtors' prison.

Obviously, the members of Parliament were also looking for new sources of wealth for England. Foremost in their minds was the export of raw materials from the colony to English manufacturers and in turn, the consumption of English finished goods shipped back to the colonies. They were especially interested in olives, grapes, medicinal plants, and mulberry trees for a silkworm industry. The English textile industry was growing immensely but the cost of raw materials, especially silk from France, was a major deterrent to profits.

King George II of England granted a charter for a colony to a group of 21 trustees. They adopted as their motto the Latin phrase "Non Sibi Sed Aliis" which is translated "not for themselves but others." The idea was to help the poor, strengthen the colonies, and promote increased trade. The seal of the colony contained a mulberry leaf and a silkworm to show the importance placed on the colony's ability to produce silk.

***Colonial Georgia Seal***

The King was also responding to religious groups pressuring him for a haven permitting religious freedom for all, except Catholics. This rendered a certain amount of moral satisfaction. It was also thought that the colony could protect South Carolina from the Spanish threat to the south. That was the primary reason for barring Catholics. It was feared their first loyalty was to the Spanish in Florida and this would expose the colony to possible attack. All in all, it was a fine plan and the settlement would be the last of the original 13 colonies.

The colony was named Georgia, to honor King George II and hopefully promote his continued interest. The trustees were not permitted to own land in Georgia and they received no salary. Eventually, there were 72 trustees, with the additional trustees being required to pay for the honor.

So it was on November 17, 1732, from Gravesend on the Thames, that the 200-ton galley ship *Anne* sailed to the new world. The ship was small, being only 74 feet long and 21 feet wide. It was laden with 114 colonists, comprising 35 families, and commanded by 36 year old James Edward Oglethorpe. A few of the colonists were able to pay their passage, but many were indentured servants who were bound to work out their passage over a five to seven-year term. At the end of that period they were promised a cow, a sow, and 50 acres. Many didn't live to receive it. Of the 114 original settlers, 50 were dead by the end of the second year in the new colony.

No one knows for sure why Oglethorpe volunteered to lead the group. Perhaps it was because he was single at the time and looking for adventure. Also, none of the other trustees had expressed an interest in being an active leader in the settlement. The charter had granted the colony the land between the Savannah River on the north and the Altamaha River on the south and westward to the Pacific Ocean. After an uneventful crossing of 58 days, the first port of call was Charleston. Only Oglethorpe disembarked. The next stop was Beaufort where all went ashore. From there Oglethorpe and a small party went southward along the coast in search of a suitable site for the colony. He was accompanied by William Bull, a civil engineer from Charleston. Bull had previously scouted the area and knew of several possible sites. They looked initially at Tybee Island but Oglethorpe was disappointed to see that it was mostly marshland. Bull mentioned a site with higher elevation on a bluff but said it was occupied by a tribe of Indians.

Navigating up the Savannah River about 15 miles, they came to the bluff. The Indians called the river Isundiga, or Bluewater. Oglethorpe's records give his reasons for choosing the site as: high ground; dry soil; fresh water from the river; and that an Indian nation, knowing the nature of the country, had chosen it for their village. Another unrecorded reason was that it was as close to South Carolina and as far away from Spanish held Florida as possible.

The boat arrived at what was known as Yamacraw Bluff and was greeted by Tomochichi, the Mico (chief) of the Yamacraw Indians. The

*Oglethorpe greets the Indians*

Yamacraws were part of the Lower Creek Indians and had been exiled and separated from the others after the Yamasee Wars in South Carolina. They had been living on the bluff since 1728. Tomochichi was accompanied by his tribe, and Mary and John Musgrove, who operated an Indian trading post called "Cowpen." The Musgroves were each half Indian and had been in the area for some time. Having been educated at white schools, they functioned as translators. All in all, the welcoming party numbered about 50.

Oglethorpe presented the Indians with a variety of gifts. He then expressed to them that as they possessed such an abundance of land, that he hoped they would permit his little group to settle on a small part of it. Tomochichi was reputed to be a great speech maker and said he hoped the English would love and protect his small tribe. When the formalities were over, permission was given for the colonists to settle undisturbed on the site selected for the town.

The town was named "Savannah," the English derivative of the Spanish "Sabina," the name of the river. Others say it was named for the grassy plains, or savannas, surrounding the town on all sides.

*Tomochichi & Toonahowi*
*Courtesy of H. Paul Blatner*

Oglethorpe returned to Beaufort for the colonists. To make the trip to the new site, they transferred to smaller boats and traveled through the inland waterway to the Savannah River. It was on February 12, 1733, that he led the settlers up the Savannah River to their new home on the bluff.

Relations with the Indians and the colonists were good from the beginning. In May of 1733, a Treaty of Friendship was signed allowing the English to settle on any lands but Sapelo, Ossabaw, and St. Catherine's Islands. These coastal islands were to remain Indian land forever. The treaty also pledged Indian support against the Spanish and the French.

The town was laid out according to a plan Oglethorpe had developed in England. It originally called for four squares of about one acre each that became central to defined wards in the town. The plan was expanded to 24 squares as the town grew. Oglethorpe personally laid out six of them during his ten years in the colony. Each ward had four trust lots with two located on the east and west sides of the squares. These were to contain public buildings and churches. On each square there were four "tythings" for the erection of the colonists' private homes, two on the north side and two on the south. Each tything lot measured 60 x 90 feet and backed up to a lane.

Those who were not indentured servants were given a tything lot in the town, five acres of garden land just outside the town, and a 44-acre farm beyond the garden lots. In return, the colonists were supposed to remain in Georgia for at least three years with the first year devoted to public works.

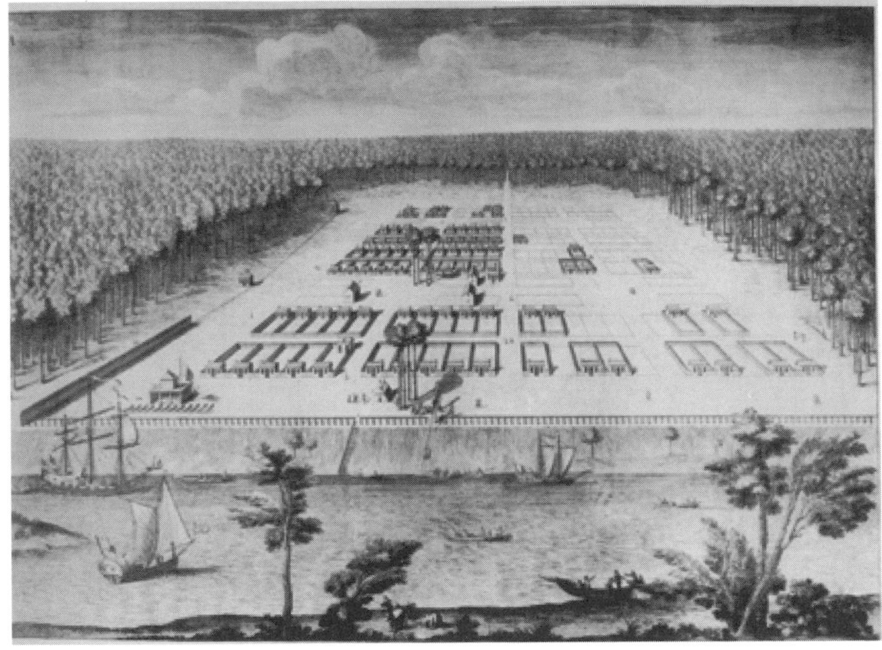

***Savannah in 1734 as drawn by colonist Peter Gordon***

They also were bound to plant 100 white mulberry trees on ten acres of their land. The leaves were to be used for feeding the silkworms.

Savannah's town plan was well suited for military defense. The squares were ideal for training and drilling troops and the streets could readily move them from one defensive post to another. The colonists lived in tents until they could construct their crude cottages. Oglethorpe pitched his tent beneath four big pine trees on the bluff. He lived there for the first year.

As the town grew, Oglethorpe assigned newcomers to what he called "outvillages." Each settler was given 50 acres of land and a house lot. He didn't own the land, it was only his to use as long as he cultivated it properly. Each settlement was fortified with cannon and the citizens were expected to stand watch on a 24-hour basis. Most of these early villages were made up of people of similar ethnic backgrounds.

The last villages were created in 1742 when the German and Swiss indentured servants completed their terms of indenture and asked for the land promised. Oglethorpe created two villages for them, Vernonburg for the

Germans and Acton for the Swiss. Vernonburg still exists today as an incorporated community on the south side of Savannah. It is near White Bluff Road on the Vernon River. White Bluff takes its name from the early reference to Vernonburg. Acton was about a mile or two northeast of Vernonburg near today's intersection of Montgomery Crossroads and Whitefield Avenue. Another settlement, west of Savannah along the Ogeechee River, was Fort Argyle that was manned by Scottish soldiers.

The colony also had settlers who had the means to pay their own passage plus bring indentured servants. They were granted 500 acres of land, which was the largest that any one person could own under the rules of the trusteeship. Among them were Thomas Causton at Ockstead, Noble Jones at Wormsloe, Thomas Parker and Henry Fallowfield at Isle of Hope, William Stephens at Beaulieu, and Roger Lacy at Thunderbolt. Bethesda Orphanage also received a 500-acre grant which it still owns.

Among the first settlers in the new colony were Sephardic Jewish immigrants of Portuguese extraction seeking to escape the Inquisition. They arrived just five months after the first colonists. Oglethorpe was ordered by the trustees not to give them land. This was despite the trustees' statements of religious freedom. When the Jews arrived there was a terrible outbreak of fever in the colony. One of them, Dr. Samuel Nunez, arrested the outbreak and in Oglethorpe's opinion, saved the colony. For this reason Oglethorpe felt he could not deny them and granted each Jewish man 50 acres of land just as he had the other settlers.

In a short time, other religious groups came to the colony. The Lutherans from Salzburg settled a few miles up the Savannah River at a place called Ebenezer. Groups of Scots and German speaking Moravians were also some of the first settlers. Early in the colony as well were the brothers John and Charles Wesley. The Wesleys were noted preachers of the gospel for the Anglican Church and the founders of Methodism. John Wesley was only 32 when he arrived in Georgia ready to convert the Indians. Charles was Oglethorpe's personal secretary and Secretary of Indian Affairs in Georgia. In 1738 Reverend George Whitefield arrived with his friend James Habersham and founded one of the nation's first orphanages at Bethesda. The need was critical because of the high death rate in the colony. It was patterned after the successful model of the Salzburger orphanage at Ebenezer a few miles upriver from Savannah.

In the early days Savannah had several prohibitions enforced. Slaves, lawyers, distilled spirits, and Catholics were all taboo. In time, each of these restrictions fell to public pressure. Although spirits were not allowed, wine, beer and ale were permitted. In fact, beer was Oglethorpe's favorite drink. Outlawing spirits led the people to erect many stills and engage in bootlegging whiskey into the colony. The lawyer prohibition was probably reflective of Oglethorpe's experience with English jails that advocated that every man should speak for himself. The slave question lingered over the colony for some time. Georgia was the only free colony without slaves, although from the beginning, the colonists had petitioned the trustees for the right to own slaves. When the colonists first settled, slave labor was borrowed from neighboring South Carolina residents to clear land for the city. The Catholic prohibition was because the English felt their allegiance might be to the Spanish in Florida and that would make the colony vulnerable to an invasion. A fifth prohibition was also considered. It was to bar any gold or silver content in clothing or furniture. However, because all the colonists were so poor, it was considered unnecessary.

***James Edward Oglethorpe***

Oglethorpe, newly promoted to General, left Savannah in 1743 never to return. He had spent only ten years in Georgia but his concern for it would last his lifetime. For ten years after his departure, the trustees continued their stewardship. Unanticipated problems continued to arise.

Formal government had never been instituted in the colony and even Oglethorpe possessed no legally mandated duties or responsibilities. In 1737 the trustees dispatched William Stephens to Georgia in the capacity of resident secretary. He was to report back to them on items of interest. His journal was subsequently published in England. In 1743 Stephens was appointed the first President of Georgia. He was succeeded by Henry Parker of Isle of Hope from 1750 to 1752, for whom Parkersburg was named. Patrick Graham was the third President and served until 1754.

Most of the colonists had been city dwellers with no knowledge of farming and they fared poorly. They complained about the restriction on the size of their holdings and the prohibition of slavery. They realized by crossing the Savannah River into South Carolina, they could get all the land, slaves, trade, and security they were unable to obtain in Georgia. As conditions reached a crisis point the trustees agreed to change the rules and slavery was permitted beginning January 1751. Labor intensive rice became a major crop and soon slaves comprised one-third of the population. Then in 1752, only a year before the charter expired, the trustees turned the colony back to the Crown. They stipulated that Georgia should not be allowed to be annexed by South Carolina. At that time the neighboring colony to the north was pressuring England to be allowed to annex Georgia.

Now it would be up to the Crown to deal with the problems. The colony thus became a province run by royal governors. Lawyers were now permitted and soon there was a flourishing bar association in Savannah. At that time the fledgling colony had 2,381 white settlers and 1,066 blacks. It contained about 200 houses, all but three of which were wooden and most painted either red or blue.

## The Royal Province

Georgia was developing a plantation economy similar to South Carolina's. The planned colony and Oglethorpe's utopian dreams were but memories. Fortunately, the design for the town plan remained. But now, only Bethesda and Wormsloe retained their acreage as original tracts. A few villages like Thunderbolt and Vernonburg and plantations like Beaulieu continued as place names. The 50 acre lots were absorbed into larger plantations. This so incensed Lord Percival, as president of the trustees, that he resigned. The original rule of no man owning more than 500 acres had been repealed in 1752 and now some landholdings were as vast as 75,000 acres. Low swampy areas previously unsuitable for farming were transformed into rice fields with the advent of slave labor.

The prohibition on slavery had been repealed due to pressures from influential Georgians like James Habersham, the colony's most successful

*A typical slave auction*

merchant and George Whitefield, the colony's best known minister. Much of the coastal island land was used for the cultivation of indigo and dry rice. Some experimentation was made in growing sea island cotton and the first cotton crop in Georgia is thought to have been planted by John Earle on Skidaway Island in 1767. Sea Island cotton was responsible for much of Georgia's agricultural success in the eighteenth century. Its long fibers didn't stick to the seeds and it was easier to harvest than short staple cotton. However, it only seemed to flourish on the sea islands and not inland where the short staple was hardier.

In 1754 John Reynolds, the first of the royal governors, arrived. Reynolds had been a sea captain in his majesty's navy. He was given broad powers and established a legislature. Noble Jones and James Habersham were among the first to serve. It is said he ran the colony in the same manner he would captain a ship, antagonizing almost everyone. He even attempted to move the seat of government from Savannah to the south side of the Ogeechee River at a place called Hardwicke. This town had been created in honor of his kinsman, Philip Yorke Hardwicke, the high chancellor of England. Fortunately, the idea stagnated and Reynolds was recalled to England and promoted to admiral in the royal navy.

The American forces led by General Benjamin Lincoln, were joined with General Lachlan McIntosh's troops at Cherokee Hill near today's Garden City. They were further strengthened by Polish Count Casimir Pulaski's cavalry and Sergeant William Jasper's regiment of the South Carolina infantry.

Admiral D'Estaing demanded surrender of the city from the British commander, General Augustine Prevost. Prevost countered by asking for a 24-hour truce. He secretly hoped that reinforcements from South Carolina would arrive and was playing for time. Although some reinforcements did get through, many were intercepted by the Americans.

***Augustine Prevost***

One British officer who did evade the blockade was Colonel John Maitland. He came with 800 fresh troops from Beaufort. Being guided by local fishermen through the little known passages of Wall's Cut and Skull Creek, he came at high tide in heavy fog and was able to evade the Americans. Upon arriving, he strode into Governor Wright's council room and announced that any man who recommended surrender would be his enemy.

Maitland was not able to enjoy his fame for long. He was ill with fever during the battle and died a few weeks later. He was buried in Colonial Park Cemetery. For many years he shared a vault with the American hero, General Nathanael Greene, until Greene's remains were transferred to his monument in Johnson Square. Colonel Maitland's remains were finally returned to his descendants in Haddington, Scotland in 1981.

The French and American armies began shelling the city to weaken the substantial fortifications installed by the British. The bombardment was ineffectual, killing only one British soldier. On October 9, 1779, the combined French and American force attacked on the west of town at the Spring Hill redoubt (barrier) guarding the Augusta Road. This spot in the British defense was considered most vulnerable to attack since Yamacraw Swamp offered cover for the Americans to within 50 yards of the fortifications.

***Battle of Savannah - October 9, 1779***

Count Pulaski suggested the Americans under Lachlan McIntosh attack the left, the French the right, and his cavalry with the primary attack up the center. The timing of the attack was uncoordinated and it seemed the British knew the point of attack long before it was initiated. It was even rumored that a Sergeant Curry from Charleston went over to the British side and revealed the American plans. This has never been documented. Actually, the British knew everything that was going on in the American camp with the help of the civilians in Savannah, who went constantly to the camp and returned to town in the evening. With that information, the British concentrated their cannon at the critical point, pouring chain and grapeshot on the Patriot forces.

The attack was extremely disjointed. Many troops were abandoned by the local guides showing them the terrain. The French forces attacked according to seniority of the regiments and within the regiments, the seniority of the company captains. This created much delay and confusion and the attack that was supposed to be launched at 4:00 a.m. was still assembling at advocating secession. Meetings were held day and night as the topic took center stage in most conversations.

Before Georgia's secession, Governor Brown ordered three of Savannah's militia units, numbering 134 men under General Alexander Lawton, to seize Fort Pulaski. Since it was defended only by an ordinance sergeant, who later joined the Confederacy, and a caretaker, the seizure was not a problem. This was accomplished soon after South Carolina seceded from the Union and even before the Confederate troops in Charleston fired on Fort Sumter.

On January 19, 1861, Georgia became the fifth state to secede from the Union. The military leaders in Savannah knew the importance of controlling the river from the sea to the town and immediately erected Fort Cheves on Hutchinson Island. Earthenwork fortifications were put in at Causton Bluff and named Fort Bartow. Fort McAllister was begun in 1861. It too was an earthenwork fortification located at the mouth of the Ogeechee River.

By November, 1861, Union forces were blocking the mouth of the Savannah River at Tybee Island. Confederate General Robert E. Lee came to Savannah to inspect coastal defenses. It was his opinion that Fort Pulaski could be defended but that Tybee Island should be evacuated. This was ordered and soon after, Union troops began work on gun emplacements on Tybee Island. From there, they had an unobstructed and undefended path to bombard Fort Pulaski. By hindsight, evacuation proved to be the wrong strategy.

The Confederate garrison at Fort Pulaski refused to surrender, believing the cannon fired from Tybee Island could not reach the fort. On April 10, 1862, a 30-hour bombardment began, using the new rifled cannon that had recently been

***Charles H. Olmstead***

developed. It soon became apparent, that resistance was futile. The Confederate commander, Colonel Charles Olmstead, surrendered. Rather than sending his men to a useless and certain death, he yielded his sword. Union troops would occupy the fort until the end of the war. The Yankees placed Savannah under a coastal blockade prohibiting any trading or commerce. This effectively stopped all goods being brought in by ship to the town. In the three years from the fall of Fort Pulaski until the coming of General Sherman. Savannah gradually starved.

The town took on a ghost town atmosphere with empty shelves and depleted stocks. Prices soared. It was said that a housewife needed a market basket to carry her money whereas her hand purse was ample to carry the purchases.

***Explosion of the Confederate gunboat Savannah***

No southern port built more ships than Savannah. Three ironclads were launched; the *Atlanta*; the *Savannah*; and the *Georgia*. With Fort Pulaski in Union hands, not only could supplies not get in but these ships could not get out. Actually the *Atlanta* did, by the way of Thunderbolt and the Wilmington River to the Atlantic. There, she ran aground and was intercepted by two Union ironclads and captured. In the *Georgia's* case, it was so heavy and unseaworthy, it had to be towed to Fort Jackson where it was moored and used as a floating battery. It was scuttled as Sherman's troops approached Savannah and still remains submerged in the river about 600 feet north of Fort Jackson. The *Savannah* was exploded by the retreating Confederate Army after it fired a parting shot at Fort Jackson, which was then occupied by Union troops.

By 1864, Georgia had supplied more troops to the cause and had suffered more casualties than any other Confederate state. In the fall of that year, Union General William T. Sherman began his march from Atlanta to the sea. The path of march was through the heart of central Georgia and to end up in Savannah. Sherman was burning everything in his path. He overran Fort McAllister below Savannah and upon hearing the news, many in the city evacuated. Those Confederate troops that remained in Savannah, under General William Hardee, left their campfires burning and spiked their cannon but still aimed them at the enemy. The navy yard and its vessels of war were also burned to prevent capture.

***William T. Sherman***

With more than 1,000 workers, comprised of slaves, navy, and militia, the retreating Confederate troops built several slippery pontoon bridges across the Savannah River and escaped into South Carolina.

On December 22, 1864, shortly after his entry into the city, Sherman sent a telegram to President Lincoln offering Savannah with its 25,000 bales of cotton as a Christmas present. Union soldiers wrote home that Savannah was the most beautiful place they had ever seen. The city was spared the torch but not a fire. Within a month of surrender, fire broke out in the downtown

*Citizens waiting for food*

ammunition depot at Granite Hall near West Broad (M.L.K., Jr. Boulevard) and Broughton Streets and more than 100 buildings were lost.

A short time after the occupation of Savannah, three ships wiggled their way up the Savannah River amid the scuttled debris of the Confederate navy. They were relief ships from Boston filled with food and supplies. A note from Mayor Lincoln of Boston accompanied the provisions and said: "The history of former friends is not forgotten. It has rather been deepened by the later trials of our nation. We remember the earlier kindness and liberality of the citizens of Savannah toward the people of Boston in the dark colonial days." The overture from the Liberty Boys during the Revolution had been repaid.

*John Gordon*

A humorous but pathetic footnote to this story is that a few of Savannah's so-called "men of substance," surrounded by gaunt women and hollow-eyed children, approached the officer in charge of the ships. They politely requested that the officer provide the necessary labor to unload the ships since they were not accustomed to such manual labor.

In April the following year, the Savannah Volunteer Guards, under General John B. Gordon of Georgia, would lead the last Confederate attack of the war near a farm in Virginia called Appomattox Courthouse.

## Reconstruction

On January 16, 1865, while still occupying Savannah, Sherman issued his famous Field Order No. 15. It confiscated the coastal islands of Georgia from their former owners and turned them over to the newly freed slaves. It prompted the memorable expression, "forty acres and a mule." Nine months later, the order was nullified by President Andrew Johnson. In spite of this, fortune was working in favor of the freed slaves. Many of the landowners of the area had either moved, abandoned the land, or been killed in the war. Land prices had fallen to two dollars an acre for farm land. Thus the free market had accomplished what Sherman had intended to do. Now, many of the freed slaves were able to acquire land for the first time.

The great plantations that were so dependent on slave labor gradually went out of business. They were caught in a vicious cycle. Slave labor was no longer available and field hands were difficult to find. Without field hands, cotton could not be produced. The plantations were unable to compete due to increasing labor costs. Many of the former rice plantations along the Savannah River were drained and sold for industrial development.

*Generals Lee and Johnston in 1870*
*Courtesy of H. Paul Blatner*

War was over and the reconstruction era began. It was a time when the most notable southern hero of the war, General Robert E. Lee, stopped in Savannah while en route to visit his father's grave on Cumberland Island, Georgia. During that time he was swamped by both an adoring populace and those friends made years earlier when he was stationed at Fort Pulaski. While in town, he and Confederate General Joseph E.

Johnston, who was then a Savannah resident, sat for the photograph that is so treasured today.

It was also a time of carpetbaggers and the beginning of the Ku Klux Klan. Many freed slaves returned to the fields as sharecroppers but many also stayed in the city. Negroes were free but they were not being assimilated into the white community. As black shanty towns grew, disease became a major problem. Lack of sanitation spawned smallpox which in turn decimated the black community.

Most blacks had never left the plantation where they were born and worked. The ability to relocate was the best exercise of their new freedom. They also knew that education was the key to a better life. Many black schools began to spring up, particularly those affiliated with churches and in 1875 a black newspaper, the Savannah Tribune, was founded.

***Savannah River - 1872***

Prior to the war it had been illegal to teach slaves to read and write. Going into the Reconstruction era, more than 90 percent of the blacks were illiterate. Alfred E. Beach, noted philanthropist and publisher of the Scientific American Magazine, donated money for an institute of learning for black Americans in Savannah.

In 1889, fire again struck Savannah. It began in the front window of Hogan's Department Store at Barnard and Broughton Streets. Driven by high winds, the flames destroyed more than 50 buildings including the Independent Presbyterian Church. Telfair Art Museum was spared only by a change in wind direction.

## Turn of the Century

*Savannah State University*

The Georgia State Industrial College for Colored Youths was begun in Athens in 1891. It transferred to Savannah the same year. By 1898, it had awarded its first degree. The school was the first state supported college for blacks in Georgia. President William Howard Taft visited the institution in 1912. Over the years the school had gone through several name changes and in 1950 it settled on the name Savannah State College. It was awarded university status in 1996.

*Racing Program*

By the turn of the century, Savannah had shifted from its dependence on agriculture. Railroads and shipping were now important and many industries had begun to locate on the old plantation sites along the Savannah River. Population of the city stood at about 50,000.

Savannah became famous as a center for auto racing during the period 1908 to 1911. In 1910 the Grand Prize Race was run and in 1911, the Vanderbilt Cup.

Cotton was falling victim to the boll weevil which moved in from

Texas and by 1924 the state had lost one-half of its crop. Production had long been declining due to the exhausted soil depleted by the replanting of the same crop. This led to a recognition of the need to diversify agriculture.

On the eve of WWI, the port became even more vital. Shipbuilders came to the port with navy contracts to build a large number of ships. Both during and after the war were periods of intense patriotism in the city. Estill Avenue, named in honor of Colonel John H. Estill of the Savannah Morning News, and Dale Avenue in Thunderbolt, were renamed Victory Drive in 1922.

***Victory Drive and Waters Avenue - Looking East***

A monument is located at the intersection of Victory Drive and Waters Avenue with the names of 113 Chatham County residents who lost their lives in the war. Palm trees were planted along the median on Victory Drive and extended 19.8 miles along a new road to Tybee Island. Each one represented a veteran of Chatham County who served his country during the war. It remains the longest palm-lined drive in the world.

At war's end and on into the roaring twenties, the jazz age was in full swing. This didn't mean everyone was happy. In fact the city council passed an ordinance outlawing jazz music. It lead, they said, to jazz dancing, jazz dressing, and jazz behavior. It was also unenforceable.

In 1923 the road to Tybee Island officially opened. It provided an alternative to taking the train that for many years, other than boats, had been the only access. Railroad service to Tybee Island began in 1887 and continued to run until 1933. In 1925, a bridge over the Savannah River at Port Wentworth was completed, giving immediate access to South Carolina. By 1929, the population of the city had grown to about 125,000. The economy was boiling at a fever pitch and Savannahians, like everyone else in the country, thought the crash of the stock market was not reflective of local business conditions. Like everyone else, they were wrong.

The following year shipping was down more than 50 percent. In 1931 there were 35 bank failures in Georgia. The Morning News and Evening Press merged their two dailies under the same management. It was a time when enormous amounts of land changed hands. It was when the last of the rice plantations along the Savannah River were parceled and sold to industrial interests. The spacious townhouses in the downtown area were divided into small apartments and became a form of tenement housing.

Savannah entered the air age with its own hero, Frank O'Driscoll Hunter, the only WWI ace from Georgia. In 1932 the city named the municipal airport, Hunter Field, in his honor. Going into WWII, Fort Stewart was also opened and Savannah became an important military location. The Eighth Air Force was inaugurated at the National Guard Armory on Forsyth Park and immediately departed for England. Their famous "Winged-8" symbol was the design of Air Force Major Ed Winter of Savannah. The Georgia Hussars, established in 1736 by General Oglethorpe, was the first American ground force to engage the Japanese in combat in the Southwest Pacific theater.

The Soldier's Social Service of Savannah, a forerunner of the U.S.O., was begun by Mrs. Thomas Hilton. It was the first organization of its kind in the country. The city was important to the war effort, both as a port and a shipbuilding center. During the war, 88 liberty ships and ten AV1 cargo ships, called "ugly ducklings," were completed at the Southeastern Shipyard on the Savannah River. Savannah lost 223 of its citizens in WWII.

## Preservation Movement

In 1946, shortly after the end of the war, Savannah was the hostess city to the International Monetary Conference. Many dignitaries were in town including the notable British economist, John Maynard Keynes and Britain's Lady Astor. Lady Astor was asked what she thought of the city. She commented: "Savannah is a beautiful woman with a dirty face."

Her words were directed to the many buildings in the downtown area that had fallen into disrepair. Also, the harbor was totally polluted from raw sewage and industrial waste and the air was even more so. Noxious fumes from paper mills

*Lady Nancy Astor*

*Old City Market on Ellis Square*

permeated the air and defiled the city. What had been some of Savannah's finest houses were now considered slum areas and Savannah was justifiably shamed.

After the war it seemed money was available only for "new" construction in downtown Savannah. There was no interest in preserving old buildings with their history and unique architectural style. One of the first battles of preservation was lost when the old city market in Ellis Square was razed in 1953 to make room for a parking garage. With this loss came the determination that sowed the seeds for the preservation movement.

Some felt Savannah's image was little more than decaying buildings and an identification with the "lost cause" of the Confederacy. This same thinking emphasized that this was the "New South" of progress, profit, and industry. The squares should be used for more functional items, like parking lots, or even cut through completely to speed traffic. They questioned the cotton heritage of the city, since so much of the wealth was built on slavery. It was felt that tourists would not come to look at a lot of old buildings.

Fortunately, there was a group not so ready to write off the squares, the cobblestones, and the houses so rich in history. As each historic building was destroyed, one by one, there was a hue and cry of protest. What was lacking was an effective organization to lend its clout to blocking the demolition of Savannah's treasures.

***Peanut Lady in City Market***

Then, it was the Davenport House's turn to face the wrecking ball. Its demolition was scheduled in 1955 by those who wanted to reclaim the brick and create yet another parking lot. In opposition, a concerned group of seven Savannah women raised the necessary $22,500 to purchase the house. It was then restored and became the impetus for beginning the Historic Savannah Foundation.

The group actively promoted restoration by private citizens by encouraging them to buy the dilapidated buildings scheduled for demolition. This transferred control from those interested in destroying these structures to those interested in saving them. The idea was to create a vibrant, taxpaying community, not a museum.

The Foundation grew to be what is today one of the most emulated and admired preservation groups in the country. An inventory of historic buildings was taken and published by the Foundation and titled "Historic Savannah." It showed that more than 40 percent of the 2,500 buildings inventoried, had architectural or historic significance.

A historic zoning ordinance was enacted by the city and the downtown area was declared a Registered Historic Landmark by the U.S. Department of the Interior. From this beginning, hundreds of buildings have been saved in the 2.5 square mile historic area. It is one of the largest urban historic districts in the nation.

Today tourism in Savannah is a huge non-polluting industry. More so, the city's structures and heritage have been preserved for its citizens and its guests to view and treasure. The history and spirit of Savannah is very much alive and bids you welcome.

# People

## Jonathan Bryan
## 1708-1788

Bryan was born in South Carolina. He was a member of Oglethorpe's expedition force against the Spaniards at St. Augustine commanding a company of volunteers from South Carolina. Bryan moved his family to Georgia in 1752 and ultimately owned several plantations. He represented the town of Savannah at the Georgia Provincial Congress in 1775 and was an active member of the Liberty Boys during this period. He was arrested by the British during their control of Savannah in 1779. They had actually gone to his plantation on the Savannah River in search of Governor John Houstoun, Bryan's son-in-law. Houstoun had sent the public records of the state there for safekeeping. The British returned without Houstoun but were able to send Bryan to prison aboard a ship off Long Island, N.Y. for over two years. During his absence, his wife died and his plantations were plundered by the British.

Bryan is said to be one of the principal founders and fathers of Georgia. Zealous in the cause of Christianity, he considered modes of worship as secondary and the great principle to be universal charity. He was very involved in the Christian movement as a Presbyterian and very supportive of George Whitefield in efforts to begin the orphanage at Bethesda. Bryan was one of the earliest members of the Union Society that has supported Bethesda through three centuries. Bryan died at his Brampton Plantation and was buried in the family cemetery. Bryan Street and Bryan County were both named in his honor.

## Comte Charles Henri-Hector Theodat D'Estaing
## 1729-1794

Admiral D'Estaing was commander of the French forces at the Battle of Savannah in 1779. Seeing the futility of his attack on the Spring Hill redoubt, he withdrew rather than prolonging the battle. D'Estaing himself was twice wounded during the charge. After the Revolutionary War he returned to France. Once there, D'Estaing became caught up in the political upheaval and

*Charles D'Estaing*

was called as a character witness for Marie Antoinette during the French Revolution. Later, with Antoinette and others, he was condemned to death on the guillotine. As his sentence was pronounced, he remarked: "When you cut off my head, send it to the English; they will pay you well for it!" He was executed at the age of 65.

## Lyman Hall
## 1724-1790

Hall studied theology at Yale and graduated in 1747. He began preaching in 1749 but abandoned the pulpit to study medicine, beginning his practice in Connecticut. In his early 30's he joined a group of Congregationalists who moved to South Carolina. Once there, they felt their land was depleted and moved again, this time to Midway, Georgia in St. John's Parish.

Being a man of education and polish, Hall rapidly became a leader in the community. Probably of all the advocates for separation from England, Hall was the hottest for the revolutionary cause.

When Georgia's Provincial Congress failed to support the other colonies, St. John's Parish, under Hall's leadership, held a convention of its own. It extended an invitation to other parishes to join with it in sending delegates to the Continental Congress. The parishes declined but St. John's was committed and elected Hall as its delegate. He was admitted to the Congress and

*Lyman Hall*

although he refrained from voting, he participated actively in the debates. When Georgia finally joined the revolutionary cause, he retained his seat in Congress and was joined by his colleagues from other parishes. Along with Button Gwinnett and George Walton, Hall was a Georgia signer of the Declaration of Independence.

Hall moved to Savannah and at the outbreak of war, his home in Savannah was seized and his rice plantation at Midway was destroyed. At that point, he moved his family north and resided there until England was defeated. At war's end he returned to Savannah and resumed the practice of medicine.

In 1783, Hall was elected governor. While serving, he made a remarkable recommendation that a grant of land be set aside for the endowment of a state supported institution of higher learning. The following year, the University of Georgia was chartered as the first state supported university in America. In 1790, Hall moved to Burke County where he again invested in a plantation but died after being there only a few months. He was in his 67th year. Hall Street and Hall County were named in his honor. He is buried in Augusta, Georgia at a monument erected for the Georgia signers of the Declaration of Independence.

## John Houstoun
## 1744-1796

*John Houstoun*

As a young man, Houstoun studied law and opened a practice in Savannah. He was one of the organizers of the liberty movement in the colony as well as the first Provincial Congress in Georgia in 1775. He was elected as a delegate to the Continental Congress but did not have the honor of signing the Declaration of Independence. It was necessary that he return to Savannah to counteract the efforts of John Zubly, who was a fellow delegate. Zubly, a Presbyterian minister and early supporter of independence, had changed his mind and was intent on defeating the movement. He was in Savannah giving fiery speeches on the merits of remaining loyal to the crown. Ultimately, he was banished from the colony.

In 1778 Houstoun was elected governor and served for a second time in 1784. During this second term an act was passed chartering the University of Georgia. He served as Chief Justice of Georgia and as Savannah's first mayor. He was married to the daughter of Jonathan Bryan, an outstanding patriot and one of the largest planters in Georgia. Houstoun died in Savannah and is believed to be buried at his home at White Bluff. Houston Street (modified form of Houstoun) and Houston County were both named in his honor.

## Frank O'Driscoll Hunter
## 1894-1982

Hunter was born in Savannah in 1894. At the outbreak of WWI, he joined the Lafayette Escadrille in France. During his service with that unit, he shot down eight planes and was the only Georgian who qualified as an air ace during the war. Hunter received five Distinguished Flying Crosses with four Oak Leaf Clusters, a Purple Heart, and a French Croix D'Guerre. In addition, he was awarded five citations for extraordinary heroism.

*Frank O'Driscoll Hunter*

In WWII, he was appointed commanding general of the Eighth Fighter Command and later of the First Air Force. Hunter Field in Savannah was named in his honor, making him the first living person to have an airport named for him. He died in 1982 at the age of 87 and is buried in Laurel Grove Cemetery.

## Johnny Mercer
## 1909-1976

*Johnny Mercer*

Mercer was born in Savannah and became one of the leaders of the Town Theater that was organized in 1925. In 1929, that group won a Belasco Award, giving it an opportunity to appear in New York City. Mercer fell in love with the city and decided to move there. While trying for an acting job, he penned his first musical composition. It was a song for the Garrick Gaieties and its popularity solidified his career as a songwriter rather than an actor.

During his career, Mercer wrote more than 800 songs and won four Oscars. He collaborated with the great song writers of the day like Jerome Kern, Hoagy Carmichael, and Henry Mancini. Memorable tunes like *"Days of Wine and Roses," "Moon River,"* and *"The Chattanooga Choo Choo"* earned Mercer a place with the all-time great song writers America has produced. Mercer was also a driving force behind Bethesda Orphanage as was his father before him. He died at the age of 67 and is buried in Bonaventure Cemetery. Johnny Mercer Theatre in the Civic Center was named in his honor.

## Mary Musgrove
## 1700-1765

Mary Musgrove was the half-breed niece of Old Brim, Emperor of the Lower Creek Indians. The Indians named her Princess Cousaponakeesa. Her father was white and possessed the means for her to be educated in Charleston. She married John Musgrove, another half Indian, and together they established the trading post of Cowpen in Savannah. The Indians were already accustomed to dealing with Europeans and were involved in an active trade of furs and skins. The Musgroves were of great assistance to Oglethorpe as interpreters, arbiters, and a source of supplies.

*Mary Musgrove*

Mary Musgrove married three times. Her last husband, The Reverend Thomas Bosomworth of Christ Church, a former commissioner of Indian Affairs, pushed her to fight in the British courts for lands designated for the Indians by treaty. The fight was successful and she was granted St. Catherine's Island for her efforts. This made her the largest landholder in Georgia in 1750. After her death in 1765, Bosomworth sold the island to Button Gwinnett. When Gwinnett died as a result of a duel with Lachlan McIntosh, Bosomworth seized the unexpected opportunity and returned to St. Catherine's with his second wife. They lived there for the remainder of his life. Both Bosomworth and Mary Musgrove are buried on St. Catherine's Island.

## James Lord Pierpont
## 1822-1893

The Pierpont brothers, James and John, were the sons of a fiery abolitionist minister in Massachusetts. John was the pastor of the Unitarian Church of Savannah and preached an unpopular abolition message to the Southern congregation. After James' wife died, he moved to Savannah from New England to join his brother as the minister of music. He courted and married Eliza Jane Purse, daughter of Mayor Thomas Purse. As the Civil War loomed, the congregation became very disenchanted with the abolition message and John returned to New York. At that point, the church was dissolved.

James remained in Savannah and wrote several popular songs, the most notable being *"Jingle Bells."* This was first copyrighted as *"A One Horse Open Sleigh,"* in 1857. When war broke out he served with the Isle of

Hope regiment in the Confederate Army. His father became a Union army chaplain and a favorite of Mary Todd Lincoln, since they both shared an interest in the supernatural. The family seemed to run in wealthy circles which is evidenced by James' nephew, J. Pierpont Morgan, gaining prominence as a famous financier and capitalist.

James asked that he be buried in Laurel Grove Cemetery in the same plot as his brother-in-law, Thomas Purse, Jr. Purse had been killed, along with Francis Bartow, at the first Battle of Bull Run. When James died in 1893 at age 71, his wishes were honored. Each grave is marked with the simple cross of a Confederate veteran.

## Sheftall Sheftall
## 1762-1847

***Sheftall "Cocked Hat" Sheftall***

Sheftall was a lawyer in Savannah and a soldier during the Revolutionary War. During the war, he was captured and suffered terrible mistreatment, spending time in prisons in Charleston and the West Indies. After the war his legal background earned him a position in Savannah as Justice of the Peace.

Obsessive patriotism emerged in Sheftall's refusal to wear any clothing other than his Continental army uniform and his tricorn hat. His hat was worn at a jaunty angle and soon earned him the nickname, "Cocked Hat Sheftall."

Every day without fail, the townspeople could see Cocked Hat as he endlessly practiced his military drills. On the wooden porch across the front of the house, he would march to one end, salute, spin smartly, and reverse his march. He was so regular, his daily marching became like another clock in the city. The floor boards of the porch at 114-116 West Broughton Street, just east of Barnard, began to show the wear from his precise military treading.

When Lafayette made his visit to the city in 1825, Cocked Hat was present on the reviewing stand, still in his old uniform. He died in 1847 at the age of 85 and is buried in Sheftall Cemetery in Savannah.

## Josiah Tattnall III
## 1795-1871

Tattnall was the son of Josiah Tattnall, Jr., governor of Georgia. He was born on the family estate of Bonaventure Plantation (now Bonaventure Cemetery), educated in England, then returned to America to join the Navy. In 1859, while he was in command of the U.S. Squadron at the East-India station, the British fleet was defeated by the Chinese at the mouth of the Pei-ho River. Tattnall sailed immediately to support the British. His act drew international attention. When he was reprimanded for breaching America's neutrality, his reply was the now famous: "blood is thicker than water." His remark played well in England and the British government expressed its thanks to President Buchanan. The incident actually helped bring about the first positive feelings between the two countries since the War of 1812.

In 1861, Tattnall resigned his commission and accepted one in the Confederate Navy. In 1862, he was assigned the defenses of the waters of Virginia with the ironclad Merrimac, renamed the Virginia, as his flagship. Several times he attempted to engage the Union ironclad Monitor, but the Monitor declined the challenge. When Confederate troops retreated from Norfolk, he burned and scuttled the Merrimac to prevent her capture.

Returning to Savannah, Tattnall took command of the Georgia naval defenses until 1863. In 1870, he was appointed to the office of Inspector of the Port of Savannah, a post he held until his death. He is buried in Bonaventure Cemetery.

## Clarence Thomas
## 1948-

Thomas was born in Pin Point, a small community outside Savannah. After a fire destroyed his home, he lived with his grandparents in Savannah attending parochial schools taught by Franciscan nuns. In 1991, as a lawyer heading the Equal Employment Opportunity Commission, he was appointed as an Associate Justice to the Supreme Court by President George Bush. Thomas was America's second black Supreme Court Justice and the second justice from Savannah. James Moore Wayne, over a century before, was the first.

*Clarence Thomas*

## Peter Tondee
## 1729-1775

The Tondee family came to Savannah from Switzerland and settled on a tything lot in the city. After the death of their parents, Peter and his younger brother Charles were apprenticed to Henry Parker of Isle of Hope. The two boys were members of the first group of orphans to occupy Bethesda. At maturity, Peter was one of three young men who formed the St. George's club, which later became the Union Society. This association provided guidance for the orphanage and financial help during times of emergency.

*Peter Tondee*

Peter worked as a carpenter and contractor and began to acquire land around Savannah. He built Tondee's Tavern at Whitaker and Broughton Streets in 1767 and it soon became a popular gathering site. The tavern was frequented by leading members of the community and became a natural meeting place to spread the fervor of revolution to the citizens of the colony. From those gatherings sprang the Liberty Boys, a group of men intent on the pursuit of American independence. Tondee acted as doorkeeper when the meetings were in session. He died in 1775 at age 46, but his wife continued to run the tavern. Unfortunately, the tavern was a casualty of the great fire of 1796. Tondee is believed to be buried in Colonial Park Cemetery.

## George Walton
## 1741-1804

*George Walton*

At 25, Walton was the youngest signer of the Declaration of Independence from Georgia. He was born in Prince Edward County, Virginia and moved to Savannah in 1769 where he began the study of law. He was admitted to the bar in 1774. Walton was an active member of the Liberty Boys that organized the Georgia Provincial Congress and erected the liberty pole in 1775. He was unanimously chosen as Secretary of the Provincial Congress and President of the Council of Safety. This group was empowered when the Provincial Congress was out of session. He was elected a delegate of the Continental Congress in 1776 and served until 1781.

When the British attacked Savannah in 1778, he served as a colonel in the Georgia Militia and suffered a broken leg from a musket ball. As he fell from his horse, he was taken prisoner. The British considered their prize so valuable they asked for at least a brigadier general in exchange. Finally, Walton was exchanged for a Navy captain in 1779. The same year he was elected governor of Georgia, the first of two terms he would serve. From 1783-1789, he served as Chief Justice of Georgia and was one of the first trustees of the University of Georgia. In 1786 he was a member of the commission to determine the boundary line between Georgia and South Carolina. Walton served as judge of Superior Court from 1790 until his death.

He was appointed in 1795 as U.S. Senator to fill the unexpired term of James Jackson. He died in 1804 and is buried in Augusta, Georgia at a monument erected for the Georgia signers of the Declaration of Independence. Walton County was named in his honor.

## Charles Wesley
## 1707-1788

***Reverend Charles Wesley***

Wesley was born in Lincolnshire, England in 1707. He arrived in Georgia in 1736 with his brother John. Charles then proceeded to Fort Frederica in his capacity as secretary to James Oglethorpe. He was there only a brief period, struggling with both his secretarial and ministerial duties. For most of his stay, he was a victim of dysentery.

Wesley unfortunately fell prey to local gossip and accused Oglethorpe of adultery with two married women. Although he withdrew the charges, things had already reached a low point for the spiritual leader. His Anglican congregation had shrunk to two Presbyterians and a Baptist. For a short period, he and his brother John switched parishes with Charles going to Savannah.

After only five months, he returned to England. There, he became a cofounder of the Methodist movement with his brother John. Since John never left the Anglican church, Charles became the first Methodist. During his lifetime he penned the words to more than 6,000 hymns including *"O For a Thousand Tongues to Sing,"* and *"Hark! The Herald Angels Sing."*

## Monuments and Markers

### Conrad Aiken Marker
**Oglethorpe Avenue median between Abercorn and Lincoln Streets**

Aiken was born in Savannah in 1889. He was a writer of novels, short stories, and critical essays but his first love was poetry. Many literary awards came his way including the Pulitzer Prize in 1930, the National Book Award in 1954, and the National Medal of Literature in 1969. Aiken held the poetry chair of the Library of Congress from 1950-1952 and was appointed Poet Laureate of Georgia in 1973.

He amassed almost every literary award that can be accorded a man of letters. During his career he produced four novels, 40 short stories, and many volumes of poetry. After a full life, Aiken returned to Savannah to a house on Oglethorpe Avenue next door to his boyhood home. Shortly before his death in 1973, the city honored him with Conrad Aiken Day. He is buried in Bonaventure Cemetery.

### Armillary Sphere
**Troup Square**

Poised on six turtles, it is an astronomical model with solid rings all circles of a single sphere. These spheres were popular during Victorian times and used to display relationships among the principal celestial circles.

*Armillary Sphere*

### Francis S. Bartow Monument
**Forsyth Park at the Confederate Monument - South End**

Originally unveiled in 1909 in Chippewa Square but moved to make room for the Oglethorpe Monument. Francis S. Bartow was a noted attorney, orator, delegate to the state convention on secession, and captain of the Oglethorpe Light Infantry. He was elected by the Georgia Secession

Convention to the Confederate Congress and actually helped shape the Confederacy. As chairman of the committee on military affairs, he insisted the gray uniform of the Savannah Volunteer Guards be adopted as the standard Confederate uniform.

Bartow was born in Savannah in 1816 and was said to be the quintessential rebel. Although a gentleman of education and means, he was nonetheless individualistic and temperamental. When Georgia seceded, he petitioned Governor Brown to allow him to lead the Oglethorpe Light Infantry to Virginia to join Generals Lee and Beauregard. When the governor refused, he offered his company's services to Confederate President Jefferson Davis, who readily accepted. Upon departing, he dashingly declared: "I go to illustrate Georgia."

*Francis S. Bartow*

On the eve of the first Battle of Bull Run, having received a scathing letter from the governor for taking his troops without permission, he wrote an even more scathing reply. It said: "Sir, in relation to myself I desire to say but little, I prefer to be judged by my actions. You make here again your common error of supposing that you are the state of Georgia, a mistake in which I do not participate. I trust if God spares my life I shall set foot again upon the soil of Georgia. With due respect, I have the honor to be your nonobedient servant."

Bartow did not survive the first Battle of Bull Run. He was shot from his horse, remounted, charged again, and was shot again, this time through the heart. With the words: "They have killed me boys, but never give it up," he died. Bartow's wife, Louisa, was in Richmond at the time and was personally advised of his death by the wife of Jefferson Davis. His remains arrived back in Savannah in July 1861, only six months after he had attended the secession convention. He was promoted to brigadier general on a posthumous basis. Bartow was a captain in May, a colonel in June, and a general in death. Of such stuff was the Confederacy made. His funeral procession was said to be one of the saddest spectacles in Savannah memory. He is buried in Laurel Grove Cemetery. Bartow County was named in his honor.

## British Defense Line Marker

### Madison Square

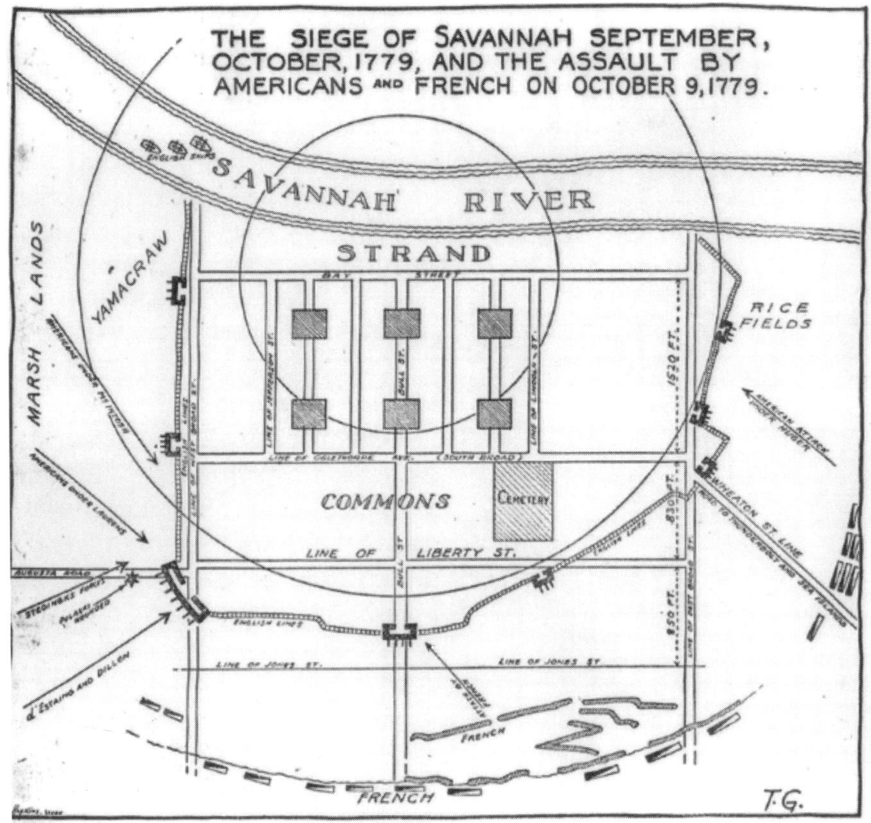


*Siege of Savannah Map*

The granite marker defines the southern line of British defense during their occupation of Savannah from 1778 to 1782. Siding with the British were English Redcoats, Scottish Highlanders, Hessians, Royal Provincials from New York, Tory Militia, armed slaves, and Cherokee Indians. On the American side were American Continentals, Grenadiers of France, Irishmen in the service of King Louis XVI, Polish Hussars, French Creoles, and black volunteers from Haiti.

After a 22-day siege ending October 9, 1779, the western defenses were assaulted by 3,500 French troops under Charles Hector Count D'Estaing and 1,500 Continental forces under General Benjamin Lincoln. Brigadier General Lachlan McIntosh commanded one attacking American column and Colonel John Laurens of South Carolina another. After three charges of unsurpassed bravery, in which Count D'Estaing was twice wounded, retreat was sounded.

Leading one of the charges at the head of his American Legion, Brigadier General Casimir Pulaski was mortally wounded. Also, among the American dead were Major John Jones of Liberty County, for whom Jones Street is named, and Sergeant William Jasper of South Carolina. This heroic assault has given to the history of Savannah and the state of Georgia a chapter in history of which none is bloodier, braver, or more noteworthy.

## William Bull Sundial

### Johnson Square

The early colonists placed a sundial in the center of the square. The current one was placed on the southern part of the square February 12, 1933 commemorating the two hundredth anniversary of the founding of Georgia.

***Bull Sundial***

William Bull of Charleston, South Carolina was born in 1683 and was serving as a surveyor for the British army when approached by Oglethorpe. Oglethorpe had come to him for assistance in locating a site for a new colony and surveying and laying out the town. His knowledge of colonial conditions led to his selection. Bull had served as Lt. Governor and member of the Commons House of South

Carolina. Once in Savannah, Bull also furnished laborers who worked for a month in building the new town. He died in 1755 and is buried in the church graveyard at Sheldon Plantation in South Carolina. Bull Street was named in his honor.

## Archibald Bulloch Marker

### Colonial Park Cemetery

Born in 1729 in Charleston, S.C., the son of a Scottish clergyman and planter. Bulloch moved to Savannah about 1750, studied law, and was admitted to practice. He was elected to the Georgia House of Commons in 1768 and served until 1773. After Governor James Wright dissolved the Assembly, he aligned himself with the Colonial Party. Bulloch's name was one of four assigned to the first call of the assemblage of patriots in Savannah on July 4, 1775. From then until his death, he was President of the Provincial Congress of Georgia and an occasional delegate and attendee to the Continental Congress. There he won the praise of John Adams for his abilities and fortitude. When Governor Wright departed the colony in 1776, Bulloch was made President and Commander-in-Chief of Georgia. He died suddenly in 1777 and was buried in Colonial Park Cemetery. Bulloch County was named in his honor. He was the great-great grandfather of President Theodore Roosevelt.

*Archibald Bulloch*

*The Celtic Cross*

## Celtic Cross

### Emmet Park at Habersham Street

Honoring those Georgians of Irish ancestry for their contributions to Savannah, to Georgia, and to the nation. The inscription reads, "To Americans of Irish descent, past, present, future. Erin Go Bragh."

## Chatham Artillery Memorial
### Emmet Park at Price Street

This unit boasts the longest continuous service of any field artillery unit in the South. It was organized in 1786 and saw its first duty in the funeral service for General Nathanael Greene. The unit provided escort for George Washington during his 1791 visit. Washington awarded the group two cannons that were captured in the British surrender at Yorktown. The Chatham Artillery served as the honor guard for Lafayette's visit in 1825. It has performed combat duty in almost every major American conflict. Thc Artillery participated in the capture of Fort Pulaski at the outbreak of the Civil War and fought later in Charleston, Florida, and North Carolina. It fought in the Spanish American War; fought Pancho Villa at the Mexican border; the Kaiser's men in France in WWI; and Hitler in Europe in WWII landing on Omaha Beach in February 1944. The memorial was dedicated in 1986 on the two hundredth anniversary of the forming of the unit. The inscription reads, "soldiers in war; patriots in peace."

*Chatham Artillery Memorial*

## Chatham County Firefighters Memorial "Big Duke"
### Oglethorpe Avenue between Abercorn and Drayton Streets

This bell was acquired by the city in 1873 and named for Fire Committee Chairman Marmaduke Hamilton. For years it hung in Colonial

*Big Duke*

Park Cemetery on a steel tower. Its primary function was to sound the fire alarm. It was moved to its current site in 1968 where it is part of "Last Alarm," a memorial to the firefighters who have died in the line of duty. It is dedicated to that unselfish organization of men and women who hold devotion to duty above personal risk, who count sincerity of service above comfort and convenience, who have given their lives protecting the homes, and property of their fellow citizens from the ravages of fire and other disasters.

## City Exchange Fire Bell

### Emmet Park west of Abercorn Street

This bell is believed to be one of the oldest in Georgia, imported from Amsterdam and bearing the date 1802. When the threat of fire was so great in the city, the bell was hung in the City Exchange Tower on the site of the present City Hall building. The tower was manned each night to watch for fires. The bell was also rung to signal the beginning of trading on the Savannah Cotton Exchange and the closing time for shops in the city. The replica of the tower was erected in 1957. On each side are urns donated to the city in 1858 by General Henry R. Jackson, the U.S. Charge d'affaires in Austria.

*City Exchange Bell*

## Confederate Monument
### Bull and Gwinnett Streets
### Center of Forsyth Park

*The Confederate Monument*

Designed by Robert Reid and erected in 1874 to honor the living and dead, who served the Confederacy. In the cornerstone there is a portion of Fort Sumter's flag, a furlough signed by General Robert E. Lee, and the flag of the 8th Georgia Regiment. The inscription on the east side of the monument reads, "Come from the four winds, O, breath, and breathe upon these slain, that they may live." It was made in Canada with Canadian materials and brought to Savannah by ship so as to never touch Yankee soil. However, when the monument reached Savannah, the memorial association was very disappointed. The monument was not at all what it expected and did not make the statement it desired. The structure contained two statues: *"Silence and Judgement."* The figure *Silence* was in the midsection of the monument and *Judgement* was at the top. The effect was not what was felt to be fitting for the Confederate dead.

George Wymberley Jones DeRenne, one of Savannah's most public spirited and generous citizens asked the association if he could be permitted to donate a bronze Confederate soldier to be placed atop the monument. The offer was accepted and in 1879, the bronze soldier by David Richards was presented to the Ladies Memorial Association, the forerunner of the United Daughters of the Confederacy. Ironically, Richards was a Northerner and the statue was cast in New York, so the pinnacle of the monument did touch Yankee soil. Today the soldier stands like a faithful sentinel, his coat torn and a bullethole in his hat, facing north against the enemy in the Southern tradition, guarding the sacred memory of the "Lost Cause." The figure of *Judgement* was dispatched to a Thomasville cemetery and *Silence* was reverently ordered to Laurel Grove to stand watch over the Confederate dead.

## Captain Denis N. Cottineau de Kerloquen Marker
### 1745-1808
### Colonial Park Cemetery

Cottineau received a commission in the Continental Navy during the Revolution commanding the slow sailing *Pallas,* a converted merchant ship with only 32 guns. He was a part of the famous naval engagement in 1779 where John Paul Jones and the *Bon Homme Richard* defeated the *Serapis.* Cottineau, by skillful seamanship forced the British ship, *Countess of Scarbrough,* to strike her colors.

He was married to the sister of the Marquis de Montalet who at the time owned the Hermitage Plantation near Savannah. Cottineau came to Savannah in early 1808 but died the same year. He is buried in Colonial Park Cemetery. As Savannah historian Thomas Gamble noted, "His grave is visible to all and recognized by few. Yet that little venerable blackened stone, which awakens so meager interest, connects Savannah with the greatest of the naval battles of the American struggle for freedom."

## Flame of Freedom
### Liberty Square

Erected and lit July 1969 by the American Legion to celebrate the 50th anniversary of its founding. The flame is an eternal memorial in honor of all men in all conflicts who fought and lost their lives in the defense of the freedom of America.

*Flame of Freedom*

*The Forsyth Fountain*

## Forsyth Fountain
### Forsyth Park

Erected in 1858, this cast iron fountain is in a design similar to the grand fountain in Paris in the *Place de la Concorde.* The twin of the fountain is in Cuzco, Peru. The pool is filled with mermen with a water nymph atop the fountain. When installed it was thought to be the largest fountain in the country.

With the exception of Pulaski's monument, it is the most visited attraction by tourists in the city. The fountain was extensively renovated in 1988 through a community effort and the perimeter within the fence of the fountain is paved with bricks carrying the names of those who donated to the project.

## Gaston Tomb

### Bonaventure Cemetery facing front gate

William Gaston was president of the Planter's Bank during the heyday of the cotton boom. He was known for his philanthropy and his generosity as a host. It was said that no stranger came to Savannah who was not welcome at Mr. Gaston's bountiful board on the northeast corner of Habersham and Broughton Streets. On a visit to New York in 1837, he died suddenly at 50 years of age. It was decided by his friends that a mausoleum should be built for him to perpetuate his spirit of hospitality.

*Gaston Tomb*

This was to be used as the "Stranger's Tomb" where visitors who died in Savannah were placed awaiting transfer to their home communities. Gaston, who had been the generous host to living strangers would be the silent host to the dead ones. "In life he entertained strangers and in death they slept with him."

The tomb was completed in 1846 in Colonial Park Cemetery and Gaston's remains were transferred from New York. After the desecration of graves in Colonial Park by Union troops during their occupation of Savannah, the cemetery fell into a neglected state. Gaston's tomb was reverently moved to its current location in Bonaventure Cemetery in 1873. Gaston Street was named in his honor.

## German Memorial Fountain

### Orleans Square

Erected in 1989 to commemorate the religious, social, agricultural, economic, and political contributions of the early German immigrants to the establishment and growth of the colony of Georgia. The fountain was

*German Memorial Fountain*

dedicated by their descendants in the German Heritage Society, the German Friendly Society, and the Georgia Salzburger Society.

## Georgia Hussars Marker
### Emmet Park at Lincoln Street

Organized in 1736, this troop of mounted rangers was raised by General Oglethorpe to patrol and protect the colony of Georgia from the Spanish and Indians. They fought at Bloody Marsh in 1742 and at the Battle of Savannah in 1779. They were assigned to the Pulaski Legion when Count Pulaski was fatally wounded leading the charge on the Spring Hill redoubt. The British six-pound cannon at this site is believed to be the only one still in Savannah that was used in the battle. The record of the Hussars during the Civil War was unsurpassed as was its service in Mexico against Pancho Villa, WWI, WWII, and Korea. The unit remained horse cavalry until 1940. From colonial times to Vietnam, the Hussars have represented Savannah in all wars. Before the unit was deactivated in 1978, it was assigned to the Georgia National Guard 214th Artillery Group, Battery B. The Georgia Hussars now exists as a hereditary organization, allowing descendants or relatives of prior Hussars to maintain membership in the organization.

*Georgia Hussars Cannon*

## Gordon Monument
### Wright Square

William Washington Gordon was born in 1796. After becoming the first Georgian to graduate from West Point in 1815, he studied law and was admitted to practice in Savannah. He became one of Savannah's early mayors.

*The Gordon Monument*

Gordon realized the feasibility of a rail system to access the crops produced in the interior sections of the state and actively promoted the concept of a railroad stretching from Savannah to Macon.

The dream was realized and he went on to become a founder and the first president of the Central Railroad and Banking Company of Georgia. He devoted his working career to that pursuit. Gordon died in 1842 and is buried at old St. Paul's Churchyard in Augusta. Gordon County and Gordon Street were named in his honor. The monument was designed by the architects Henry Van Brunt and Frank M. Howe and completed in 1883.

## Little Gracie
### Bonaventure Cemetery

Gracie Watson was the only child of W.J. Watson, the manager of the Pulaski Hotel at the height of its prestige. She was a delight to both Savannahians and hotel guests. Gracie died in 1889 when she was only six years old. There are still reports of a small girl in period dress who is seen occasionally in the basement of Morrison's Cafeteria at Bull and Bryan Streets where the

*Little Gracie*

Pulaski formerly stood.

Her parents commissioned a sculpture of Gracie from John Walz, who had just opened a studio on Bull Street. The statue is sculpted in Italian marble. One of the features is a carving of a sawed off tree stump representing an interrupted young life. After her death her father assumed the management of the DeSoto Hotel but ultimately left Savannah for good. Gracie was left alone at Bonaventure. Visitors to her grave often put flowers in her lap so she will know she is still loved and not alone.

## Nathanael Greene Monument

### Johnson Square

Greene was born in 1742 to a Quaker family, the son of a prosperous Rhode Island forge owner. His interest in the military led to his eventual expulsion from the pacifist Quaker church. Greene volunteered for the army at Cambridge, and rose from private to major general.

*Nathanael Greene Monument*

When war with Britain seemed imminent, he organized a company called the Kentish Guards. After the Battle of Lexington, the Guards set out for Boston to aid the American cause. The Massachusetts governor, a British Loyalist, recalled the Guards but Greene and three others continued on to Boston.

Greene served during the siege of Boston as a brigadier general and later as a major general he commanded the army of occupation in Boston. When George Washington was camped at Valley Forge, he was joined by Greene to bolster his forces. Washington recognized Greene's talent for

*Nathanael Greene*

assembling and conserving military supplies and for his diplomacy in removing intercolonial jealousies. At Valley Forge, on Christmas eve in 1776, Greene led the left column, the position that insured not only the victory over, but also the capture of, the Hessian detachment.

In 1780, he was chosen by Washington to be his Chief of Staff and second in command and was assigned all troops between Delaware and Georgia. Greene ultimately became the leader of American forces in the South. His ensuing campaign thwarted Cornwallis and ensured the patriots' success at Yorktown. More than any other commander, Greene was instrumental in freeing Georgia from British occupation.

After the war he was rewarded by the gift of Mulberry Grove Plantation about 12 miles above Savannah on the Savannah River. Unfortunately, he only enjoyed his new home for a short time. One midsummer day he was stricken with a sunstroke at William Gibbon's neighboring plantation, never to recover. His treatment consisted of being bled, then blistered about the temples, followed by the taking of more blood. He died June 19, 1786 and was buried in Colonial Park Cemetery. He was only 44.

The Marquis de Lafayette, who came to the aid of the Americans during the Revolutionary War, laid the monument's cornerstone on March 21, 1825. At the dedication ceremony he said: "a great and good man to whose memory we are paying a tribute of respect, affection, and regret has acted in our revolutionary contest a part so glorious and so important that in the very name of Greene are remembered all the virtues and talents which can illustrate the patriot, the statesman, and a military leader."

His exact resting place was a matter of doubt and speculation for many years. The remains were finally found in the Graham vault in Colonial Park Cemetery in 1901. On November 14, 1902, his remains, along with those of his son, George Washington Greene, were reinterred at the Greene Monument in Johnson Square. It is a 50-foot white marble obelisk designed by the well-known architect, William Strickland. The monument was completed in 1830. Greene County and Greene Square were named in his honor.

## Button Gwinnett Memorial
### Colonial Park Cemetery

Gwinnett was one of the three signers of the Declaration of Independence from Georgia. Born in England in 1735, the son of a clergyman, he came to Savannah in 1765 and entered the export business. His wife Ann joined him in 1767. They had three daughters but only one, Elizabeth, survived to maturity.

*Button Gwinnett Memorial*

The Gwinnetts purchased St. Catherine's Island from the Reverend Thomas Bosomworth after the death of Mary Musgrove. Being in close proximity to Midway, he developed a close friendship with Dr. Lyman Hall, who also had a plantation in the area. Through that association, he gained an interest in politics. St. Catherine's was purchased entirely on credit and by 1773, Gwinnett's creditors forced him to sell the island to pay his debts. After the sale, he moved his family to Savannah.

On February 2, 1776, Gwinnett, Dr. Lyman Hall, and George Walton were chosen as three of Georgia's delegates to the Continental Congress. After the death of Archibald Bulloch Gwinnett, Gwinnett was subsequently appointed interim governor. In that position, he commanded the Georgia Militia while General Lachlan McIntosh, a Scottish native and prominent military figure, led the Continental forces in the state. Gwinnett and McIntosh had long been good friends but McIntosh refused to acknowledge Gwinnett's authority as commander of all forces in Georgia. Problems developed between the two and contributed to the failure of an attempt to invade Florida in 1777. Each blamed the other and personal animosities developed.

*Gwinnett-McIntosh Duel*

Gwinnett also received a confidential communication from John Hancock that McIntosh's brother George was aiding the British. Gwinnett had George arrested and placed in irons. He was later tried and released by the Continental Congress.

The Council elected John Adam Treutlen as permanent governor and called both Gwinnett and McIntosh before them to explain the Florida fiasco. Gwinnett gave such a polished account of his actions he was absolved from all blame. McIntosh was furious. He called Gwinnett "a scoundrel and lying rascal." According to the custom of the time, Gwinnett sent McIntosh a challenge requesting that he meet him early on the morning of May 16, 1777.

The duel was held in a meadow on land owned by Governor Wright. It has been described as being on the north side of the road leading to Thunderbolt about a half mile from the center of the city. This would indicate somewhere

*Button Gwinnett*

southeast of the intersection of Liberty and Wheaton Streets. The men agreed to fire from four paces, or about 12 feet. They faced each other and at the signal fired simultaneously. Gwinnett was shot above the knee and suffered a bone fracture. McIntosh was shot through the leg but the wound was not serious. He asked Gwinnett if he wished to stand for another shot. Gwinnett said, "Yes, if they will help me up." The seconds, Colonel James Habersham, Jr. for McIntosh and George Wells for Gwinnett, objected and McIntosh was assisted to where Gwinnett had fallen and the two shook hands.

Three days later, on May 19, 1777, Gwinnett died of gangrene. Dr. Lyman Hall, fellow signer of the Declaration of Independence was among those who mourned. He wrote: "O Liberty, why do you suffer so many of your faithful sons, your warmest votaries, to fall at your shrine." Public sentiment against McIntosh was so great that he left Georgia for two years, joining at Valley Forge, the army of George Washington, where he distinguished himself.

Gwinnett remains a man of mystery. No ones knows for sure the date or place of his birth. Some think he grew up in Wales while others feel it was in Gloucester, near Birmingham, England. There is no verifiable portrait, even the one depicted here, so no one knows for certain what he looked like. His signature is now a collector's item with only a limited number known to exist. He is buried in Colonial Park Cemetery only a pistol shot away from his former foe, General McIntosh. Gwinnett Street and Gwinnett County were named in his honor.

## James Habersham Marker
### 1712-1775
### Colonial Park Cemetery

He came to Savannah from Yorkshire, England to begin Bethesda Orphanage with George Whitefield. Habersham was the administrator and educator and Whitefield was the preacher and fund raiser.

In 1744, Habersham resigned

*James Habersham*

as head of Bethesda to open a commercial firm with Colonel Francis Harris called Harris and Habersham. From this beginning, they established a large trade with the northern colonies, England, and the West Indies. The firm constructed the first wharf on the Savannah River capable of servicing seagoing vessels. Habersham raised and exported the first cotton to be shipped from America. After the repeal on the prohibition of slavery, he developed a large rice plantation in Savannah. The plantation was named Silk Hope although the fortune was made in rice.

In 1754, King George II appointed him Secretary of the Province and a member of the Governor's Council. In 1767, he was elected President of that body. When Governor James Wright temporarily left Savannah in 1771, he recommended Habersham as his replacement. He spoke of Habersham as a firm friend and a very worthy and honest man. Habersham became acting governor and commander-in-chief of Georgia.

He resisted the rising tide of revolutionary spirit and dissolved the General Assembly when it elected as speaker a man distasteful to the crown. Habersham's burdens as acting governor and as manager of his own extensive business interests and properties, as well as temporary manager of governor Wright's eleven plantations, were too much for his strength. With the return of governor Wright in 1773, Habersham, his health much impaired, went north for a change of climate.

Near the end of his life, he was in great distress of mind that public affairs should have taken the revolutionary turn he so much dreaded. His anguish was arrayed in his statement of his own case, "father against son, and son against father." He died in New Brunswick, New Jersey in 1775, a refugee from his home state of Georgia which was primed for revolution. He is buried in Colonial Park Cemetery. Habersham Street was named in his honor.

## James Habersham, Jr. Marker

**1745-1799**

**Colonial Park Cemetery**

James Jr. was the eldest of three sons of James Habersham. He was a merchant and planter in Savannah and possessed a quiet manner. He was often referred to as "the gentleman of the family." He had barely begun a political career in the Colonial Assembly when the Revolution erupted. At first he supported his father's position of loyalty to the crown and was in opposition to his brother Joseph's rebellious activitics. Following the death of his father, he aligned himself with his brothers and the moderate revolutionary forces in Savannah. As a merchant and a planter at Silk Hope Plantation in Savannah, he actively opposed the revenue act of Parliament in 1775. He served in the early assemblies of revolutionary Gcorgia and was active in outfitting privateers to bring supplies to the state. When the British overran Savannah in 1778, he escaped with family and slaves to South Carolina, later moving to Virginia.

After the war, he returned to Savannah. His career as a revolutionary moderate illustrates the ambivalent position of many second generation offspring of prominent early Georgia settlers. Habersham went on to serve as speaker of the General Assembly in 1782 and again in 1784. He also served on the Board of Trustees of the University of Georgia that was founded in 1785. He was frequently in poor health and died of fever at the age of 54.

## Joseph Habersham Marker
### 1751-1815
### Colonial Park Cemetery

Joseph was the second son of James Habersham. He was educated at Princeton and was an ardent espouser of the American cause, even though his father remained loyal to the crown. The family division was typical of what was happening in Georgia at the time. He was a member of the Liberty Boys that led the rebellion in Georgia. Habersham took a leading part in the first overt act of war in Savannah by capturing the British powder magazine and a vessel from London loaded with military goods.

***Joseph Habersham***

He served as a colonel in the Continental Army during the Revolutionary War. Early in the conflict, Joseph volunteered to place Sir James Wright, the Royal Governor, under house arrest. This was only five months after the death of his loyalist father. As Governor Wright sat at the table with his Council, Habersham passed the sentry at the door, placed his hand on Wright's shoulder and said, "Sir James, you are my prisoner." All present thought Habersham was supported by a large military body and the Council, fearing a similar fate, fled. Dr. William Bacon Stevens, Bishop of Pennsylvania, said: "This daring event was one of the most deliberate and successful in the history of the war. For a youth of twenty-four, unarmed and unsupported, to enter the mansion of the Chief Magistrate and at his own table amid a circle of the councilors to place him under arrest, is an act of heroism ranking with the most brilliant exploits in American history."

After the war, he served as a delegate to the Continental Congress and was a member of the convention that ratified the U.S. Constitution. Later, he served as mayor of Savannah and speaker of the Georgia General Assembly. His last public service was as Postmaster General of the U.S., appointed by George Washington in 1785. When President Thomas Jefferson invited him to become Treasurer of the U.S. in 1801, he interpreted the offer as a request for his resignation as Postmaster and surrendered his post.

He returned to Savannah and resumed his commercial career. In 1802, he became president of the Savannah branch of the Bank of the U.S., a position he was holding at the time of his death in 1815. He is buried in Colonial Park Cemetery. Habersham County was named in his honor.

## John Habersham Marker
### 1754-1799
### Colonial Park Cemetery

John was the youngest son of James Habersham and had inherited Dean Forest Plantation from his father. He served as a major of the Continental Army and was twice taken prisoner during the Revolutionary War. After the war he was elected a member of the Continental Congress in 1785. He was the first collector of customs for the port of Savannah and one of the early trustees of the University of Georgia. He also served as a commissioner in the convention which established the boundary between Georgia and South Carolina. He died in Savannah only a few months after his eldest brother and just before his 45th birthday. He is buried in Colonial Park Cemetery.

## Sergeant Jasper Monument
### Madison Square

William Jasper was born in 1750 in the vicinity of Georgetown, S.C. and died at the Battle of Savannah in 1779. He was recruited by General Francis Marion (the Swamp Fox) in June 1775 for service in the Second South Carolina Infantry. A year later, he distinguished himself in the battle for Fort Moultrie on Sullivan's Island in the Charleston Harbor.

*Sergeant Jasper Monument*

During the British bombardment of the fort, the American flag was shot down. The other two American forts, believing it was a sign of surrender, held their fire. Jasper, seizing the moment, leaped over the embankment, and recovered the flag. He then tied it to a cannon sponge staff, sprang to the parapet amid shot and shell, and raised the colors for all to see.

For his deed, Governor Rutledge presented him with a sword and offered him an officer's commission. He accepted the sword but refused the commission on the grounds that he was not qualified to be an officer, since he was unable to read and write.

During the Battle of Savannah, at the charge of the Spring Hill redoubt (barrier), Jasper's regiment broke through the British line and attempted to plant the regimental flag. The colors, carried by Lt. Bush were shot down and Jasper went forward under heavy fire and raised them again. He was struck in the chest and mortally wounded. As the shot pierced his body he murmured, "I have got my furlough." The dying sergeant asked that his sword be sent to his father. Jasper was buried in a mass grave west of Savannah with hundreds of other Continental militiamen, French, and Irish soldiers. All had sacrificed their lives in a fruitless assault. Jasper Counties in both South Carolina and Georgia were named in his honor.

The cornerstone for the monument was laid October 9, 1879, the centennial of the Battle of Savannah. The 15 1/2 foot bronze statue was designed by the sculptor Alexander Doyle of New York. The monument was unveiled in 1888. General John B. Gordon delivered the oration and President and Mrs. Grover Cleveland were among the guests of honor.

The base relief panels on the north, west, and east sides represent three significant episodes in Jasper's revolutionary career. First the rescue of the flag at Fort Moultrie in Charleston, South Carolina. Second, the liberating of the American prisoners near Savannah and third, the dying hero's last moments after the attack in the Battle of Savannah, October 9, 1779.

## Jasper Spring Marker

### Augusta Road and Lynes Parkway

Sergeant William Jasper became a notorious guerrilla fighter during the Revolutionary War, leading small patrols behind the enemy's lines and even capturing troops sent out to capture him. As a scout he was adventurous, trustworthy, and loyal. He was said to be the master of disguise and able to alter his appearance at will. He was also admired for his cunning and bravery.

*Jasper Spring*

When the British were in control of Ebenezer, they sent several prisoners, bound and guarded to Savannah for trial and execution. Jasper and Sergeant John Newton followed the patrol for many miles. When in sight of Savannah, the patrol tied their prisoners to trees and left their rifles stacked and guarded while they went to drink from a spring. Jasper and Newton sprang from concealment, shot the two guards, grabbed the muskets, shot the soldiers, and rescued the prisoners. The two soldiers with their liberated prisoners and British captives crossed the river and rejoined their army at Purysburg. The spring has since been called, "Jasper Spring."

Jasper was killed at the Battle of Savannah. Afterwards, Sergeant Newton retreated with General Lincoln's forces to Charleston. He was taken prisoner after Charleston fell and died of smallpox aboard a prison ship in 1780. Newton County was named in his honor.

## Jewish Burial Plot Marker

### Oglethorpe Avenue median at Bull Street

*First Jewish Burial Ground*

Designates the original 1733 burial plot allotted by James Edward Oglethorpe to the Savannah Jewish community. The marker was erected by the trustees of the Mordecai Sheftall Cemetery Trust. Verification was made of 16 persons but there are doubtless many more interred whose names are not now known.

## Liberty Ship Marker

### Morrell Park on River Street

The armed schooner *"Liberty"* was the first American naval vessel officially commissioned by the Provincial Congress. The Liberty was commanded by Oliver Bowen and Joseph Habersham and carried 10 carriage guns and 50 men. She flew the Liberty flag, a white banner with a red border and the motto, "American Liberty," imprinted on the field in large red letters. The schooner sailed in 1775 from the port of Savannah and made the first ordered seizure in southern waters when she captured the British vessel *Phillipa* near Tybee Island. Of the 6.5 tons of gunpowder seized, over one-half was sent north for use by the other colonies. Bowen and Habersham went on to command the Georgia Continental Navy and the first Continental Battalion respectively.

## Lachlan McIntosh Marker
### 1727-1806
### Colonial Park Cemetery

*Lachlan McIntosh*

McIntosh was born in Inverness, Scotland but came to Georgia with his brothers, George, William, and John at an early age. They were the sons of John MackIntosh who settled with a group of Scottish Highlanders on the Altamaha River near Darien in 1736. Lachlan received part of his schooling at Bethesda and later served as a cadet in Oglethorpe's regiment. He and his brother William fought with Oglethorpe against the Spanish at Bloody Marsh on St. Simon's Island during their younger years.

At the outbreak of the Revolutionary War, the McIntosh family was wealthy and controlled large plantations near Darien. These were lost in the Revolution. After the duel with Button Gwinnett, it was thought best that he leave Savannah. McIntosh was transferred by Governor Treutlen to Valley Forge to serve under George Washington. Not only did Gwinnett's widow blame McIntosh for the death of her husband, many others in Savannah did as well. Washington was glad to have a man of McIntosh's ability and described him as an officer of great worth and merit.

McIntosh returned to Savannah and served as a commander during the unsuccessful siege in 1779. He requested that his wife and children be permitted to leave the city. British General Prevost refused, so McIntosh had to endure the ordeal of knowing his family was in harm's way during the long bombardment. His military career in the American Revolution ended with his capture after the fall of Charleston in 1780.

General McIntosh Boulevard in Savannah was named in his honor and McIntosh County was named to honor the contributions of the McIntosh family. He is buried in Colonial Park Cemetery.

## Lafayette McLaws Monument

### Forsyth Park at the Confederate Monument - North End

McLaws was born in Augusta in 1821 and graduated from West Point in 1842. He married a niece of General Zachary Taylor and then served under Taylor in the Mexican War. McLaws participated in hard fighting on the Texas frontier and also in Monterey. From there he joined General Winfield Scott's army and assisted in the siege of Vera Cruz. When Georgia seceded, McLaws resigned his commission and offered his services to the Confederacy. He was promoted to brigadier general in 1861 and participated in all the Maryland and Virginia campaigns and commanded a division at Gettysburg. He was transferred to Georgia in 1863 and took an active part in obstructing General Sherman's "March to the Sea." His division was evacuated from Savannah using the pontoon bridges across the Savannah River to elude Sherman as he entered the city.

*Lafayette McLaws*

McLaws retired as a major general. After the war he returned to Savannah and entered the insurance business. While in Savannah, McLaws also served as collector for the Internal Revenue Service and postmaster. He died in 1897 and is buried in Laurel Grove Cemetery.

## Marine Monument

### Bull and Gaston Streets

Dedicated by General A.A. Vandergrift, Commandant of the U.S.

Marine Corps on November 11, 1947 to honor the Marines from Chatham County who gave their lives in WWII, Korea, and Vietnam.

## Merchant Marine Memorial

### Rousakis Plaza on River Street

A large ship's anchor on display to honor the merchant seamen whose lives have been lost at sea. Dedicated by the Savannah Propeller Club.

## Moravian Marker

### Lafayette Square

The Moravians arrived in 1735 on the same ship that brought John Wesley, who was very impressed with their piety. Their original home was in Moravia which is today a part of the Czech Republic. The Moravians set up a school at Irene Mound (near Garden City) to educate the Indians. They were avid evangelists and the other colonists did not approve of some of their religious practices. They refused to bear arms, even for defense.

Feelings against them became bitter and there were threats against their lives if they didn't share in the defense of the colony. Probably because of all their differences, the Moravians announced plans to join another group in Bethlehem, Pennsylvania. Fellow citizens of the town refused to allow them to leave until all debts were paid. Gradually the debts were paid off and by 1740, all the Moravians had moved.

The marker was presented to the city by the Wachovia Historical Society of Winston-Salem, North Carolina.

## Flannery O'Connor Marker

### 207 E. Charlton Street

Flannery O'Connor is considered to be one of the best short story writers of American birth. She was born in Savannah in 1925 and spent her formative years in the house on Charlton Street. In 1938, she moved to Milledgeville where she graduated from the Women's College of Georgia in 1945. Many of her stories were reminiscent of her childhood in Savannah. She won three O'Henry awards for the best short story of the year and the

National Book award in 1972 for her collected stories. It was felt the most important tradition influencing O'Connor's writing was her avowed Roman Catholicism. This belief established her vision of the human condition and enabled her to reach beyond her regional ties to a universal audience. She died in 1964 at the age of 39 and is buried in Milledgeville.

## Oglethorpe Monument

### Chippewa Square

James Edward Oglethorpe was born in London on December 21, 1696, the son of a knight whose family traced its lineage back to Nathanael the Confessor, the last of the Saxon kings. He was the seventh of nine children. After attending Eton and Oxford, he entered military service. At the age of 26, he was elected to Parliament. It was a post he would hold until he was 59.

*James Edward Oglethorpe Monument*

Oglethorpe's Parliamentary service gave him a good overview of the social problems of the time. A friend, Robert Castell, was incarcerated in debtors' prison due to an unsuccessful publishing venture. Castell died of smallpox while in prison. This injustice made a lasting impression on Oglethorpe and while in Parliament he headed a committee to study the deplorable conditions in prisons. Through their efforts they were able to implement some improvements.

Castell was an architect and some feel that he was the creator of the Savannah town plan using squares. In his book, "Villas of the Ancients," he called for a city showing a plan utilizing the square concept.

After spending ten years in the Georgia colony, Oglethorpe returned to England in 1743 to face charges from one of his officers. A lieutenant colonel charged him with false promises of payment to officers. Although Oglethorpe was acquitted, he never returned to the colonies. He did however remain in the British Army. Oglethorpe stayed in England and in 1745 married Elizabeth Wright, heiress of Cranham Hall.

He was once offered the governorship of South Carolina but refused. During the Revolutionary War, Oglethorpe was too old to take an active part in the conflict. Regardless of his age, many felt his sentiments were that he could never fight against Englishmen nor could he bear arms against the very colony he founded.

In later years, he became a literary figure and developed a close association with writers Samuel Johnson, James Boswell, and Oliver Goldsmith. Oglethorpe died in 1785 and was buried at Cranham in a simple grave. He was the only founder of a colony to live to see it become a part of the United States. Oglethorpe County, Avenue, and Square were all named in his honor.

The statue was designed by Daniel Chester French, with the base designed by Henry Bacon. Other works of French are the Minutemen of Concord and the Lincoln Memorial in Washington, D.C. The monument was unveiled in November 1910. The statue is 15 feet tall, attired in the full dress of a British general of the period, sword in hand, alert and ready for action or counsel. At his feet is a palmetto frond. Four lions at the corners of the base hold shields on which appear respectively the coat of arms of Oglethorpe, the seal of the colony of Georgia, the seal of the state of Georgia, and the seal of the city of Savannah. The monument is also inscribed with a portion of the charter of the trustees establishing the colony of Georgia. Oglethorpe faces southward to keep an eye out for the Spanish. Many have expressed that he should face City Hall to keep an eye on the politicians.

*Oglethorpe Bench*

## Oglethorpe Bench

**North side of Bay Street**
**West of City Hall**

The site of Oglethorpe's field tent for his first night on Georgia soil and his initial headquarters in Georgia. It is also the site of the colonists first landing in Savannah.

## Old Harbor Light

**Emmet Park at East Broad Street**

Erected as a beacon light by the U.S. Government in 1858 to guide ships into the harbor. Its purpose was also to guide mariners away from the vessels scuttled by the British in 1779 to close the harbor to French naval forces, allies to the Americans. During that siege, the British warship *Truite,* shelled this area of Savannah from her anchorage in Back River opposite this point.

To avoid the wrecks, the ships would line up the Savannah light with the Fig Island light across the river and then bear for the Fig Island light. The cast iron beacon stands 77 feet above the water level and is illuminated by gas.

*Old Harbor Light*

## Olympic Flame

**River Street and East Broad Ramp**

This cauldron was lit with the original Olympic flame from Olympia,

*Olympic Flame*

Greece at the Savannah opening ceremony in 1996. It burned throughout the centennial games in Savannah, the site of the Olympic yachting events. The five fluted columns on round bases represent the five Olympic rings and the fluted slice of a classic column symbolizes the Olympic Greek heritage. The six sails represent the Olympic yachting events and the copper flame replaces the billowing real flame. The sculpture was created by Georgia artist Ivan Bailey.

## Pulaski Monument
### Monterey Square

Casimir Pulaski was born in 1748 in a Poland struggling for independence against Russia. In 1768, Pulaski joined in active rebellion with his father to combat the foreign domination of Poland through Stanislaus II. The Polish rebellion was crushed and Pulaski's estates were confiscated. He fled to Turkey, then France, ending up in Paris as a penniless exile. He was put in touch with Benjamin Franklin who was looking for military expertise against the British in America. Poland's loss was America's gain. Franklin wrote to George Washington who welcomed Pulaski's aid.

*Casimir Pulaski*

He proved his merit in Pennsylvania before turning south. After the battle of Brandywine in 1777, he was appointed brigadier general and placed in charge of the cavalry. His cavalry acted in unison with General Anthony Wayne in scouting for supplies for the famished troops at Valley Forge. The following year he organized an independent corps of cavalry and light infantry known as Pulaski's Legion. In February 1779, he was ordered to support General Benjamin Lincoln's army that was moving to Savannah to oppose the British General Augustine Prevost.

It was at the battle of Savannah that Pulaski was mortally wounded in the groin on October 9, 1779. He was leading the Legion astride his black charger against the Spring Hill redoubt (barrier). The British, out of respect for Pulaski's courage, held their fire until he was carried from the field. The grapeshot was removed by Dr. James Lynah of South Carolina and is on display at the Georgia Historical Society in Hodgson Hall. Pulaski died two days later after the wound developed gangrene.

There is a controversy about his death and burial. Some say he was evacuated from Savannah after the battle and died aboard the ship *Wasp* and was buried at sea. Others say he was carried to the ship but was too ill to sail and was brought to Greenwich Plantation near Thunderbolt, where he died. Acting on that presumption, a grave at Greenwich was opened and its remains reinterred in a metallic case at the Pulaski Monument. There has always existed doubt as to whether the remains are those of Pulaski or another Polish officer. As a compromise, they were recognized as those of Savannah's unknown soldier who gave his life for American independence.

***Pulaski Monument***

Recent advances with DNA cell testing have given optimism too finally determining whether the remains are those of Pulaski after all. When the monument was dismantled for cleaning and repair in 1996, the bones from the metallic case were removed and tested. Enough DNA was recovered from the teeth to look for a possible match. The remains of Pulaski's great-niece have been located in Poland and hopefully a comparison will resolve the mystery.

The cornerstone for the Pulaski Monument was originally laid in Chippewa Square by the Marquis de Lafayette during his visit to Savannah in 1825. It was moved to Monterey Square and the monument was dedicated in 1853. It was constructed of Italian marble and sculpted by Polish born, Robert Eberhard Launitz. In Launitz's description "the monument is surmounted by a statue of liberty embracing with her left arm the banner of the stars and stripes while her right hand is extending the laurel wreath. The love of liberty brought Pulaski to America. For love of liberty he fought and for liberty he lost his life, thus I thought that liberty should crown his monument and share with him the homage of the free." Pulaski has been called the father of American cavalry. Fort Pulaski, and Pulaski Square and County were all named in his honor.

## Salzburger Monument

### Emmet Park between Lincoln and Abercorn Streets

The monument depicts a Salzburg family in flight and bears these words in German and English: "Denied their religious freedom, they were forced to flee their homeland." The first 37 Salzburgers to come to Georgia landed at this site in 1734. They were given temporary shelter by Oglethorpe before moving to their new home in Ebenezer in what is now Effingham County. The monument was dedicated by the Georgia

*Salzburger Monument*

Salzburger Society. The sculptor was Anton Thuswaldner.

*Scottish Memorial*

## Scottish Memorial

### Oglethorpe Avenue median at Bull Street

The inscription reads "Tyrants Fall and Every Foe - Liberty's in Every Blow," In memory of our Scottish forebears whose valor inspired these immortal lines by Robert Burns. The marker was dedicated in 1987 to commemorate the 250th anniversary of the St. Andrew's Society of Savannah.

## Savannah Police Officers Memorial

### Oglethorpe Avenue median at Habersham Street

This is a statue of a bronze uniformed policeman on a pedestal facing west. The inscription reads "Above and Beyond, Lest We Forget," dedicated to the memory of Savannah Police Officers who gave their lives in the line of duty.

*The Georgia Volunteer*

## Spanish-American War Monument

### Bull Street and Park Avenue

This 8.5 foot bronze statue of an American soldier with his rifle commemorates those Georgians who gave their lives in the Spanish-American War. It is called by many "The Georgia Volunteer" and by others simply, "The Hiker." The sculptor was Theo Alice Ruggles Kitson. The war was the first major American conflict since the Civil War and succeeded in melding Northern blue and Southern gray — into khaki. Savannah served as a major embarkation point to Cuba.

## Tomochichi Monument
### Wright Square

Tomochichi was born somewhere in the South about 1650. We know that his tribe occupied Yamacraw Bluff when the colonists arrived in 1733. He agreed to allow the colonists to settle on the bluff and move his tribe to a site four miles upriver. It was located in what became Brampton Plantation and is a part of present day Garden City.

A tract of land several square miles in size was reserved exclusively for the Indians. The site was near "Irene Mounds," an ancient Indian ceremonial complex containing a large number of skeletal remains. The Indians did not dwell on the mound site itself as they considered it haunted. Tomochichi erected a house in the English style and the Musgroves relocated their trading post to be near the Indians.

*Tomochichi Monument*

In 1734 Oglethorpe took Tomochichi, his wife Senauki, his nephew Toonahowi, and selected other chiefs of neighboring tribes to England to meet the King. John Musgrove accompanied them as interpreter. The group was greeted with much fanfare by King George II, Queen Caroline, and the Archbishop of Canterbury. Tomochichi presented the king with feathers from a bald eagle emphasizing they came from the swiftest of birds and were a sign of power. It is the first documented instance of the eagle's role as an American symbol.

One of the chiefs died of smallpox while in England, becoming the first American Indian buried on English soil. During their stay, Tomochichi's portrait was painted by several artists. He was especially honored by Lord Percival, Earl of Egmont, who presented him with a silver snuffbox. He expressed difficulty with the logic of why houses in England were built to outlast the men who lived in them. Oglethorpe finally took the party to his country estate just so they could rest and not be on display. After about four months, the group returned to America.

*Nellie Kinzie Gordon*

On October 5, 1739, Tomochichi died and the tribe abandoned the village at Irene Mounds, never to return. Tomochichi had asked to be buried among the colonists and his wishes were honored. Oglethorpe was a pallbearer and he was given all the trappings of a state funeral. The silver snuffbox was around his neck and buried with him. His grave was located in the center of Wright Square with a pyramid of stones erected over the spot.

When the Gordon Monument was placed in the center of the square in 1882, a monument for Tomochichi was placed at the present location. Nellie Kinzie Gordon headed a group to erect a suitable marker and wrote to a quarry in Stone Mountain Georgia requesting a proposal.

The owner was so impressed with her plea that he offered the largest piece of granite in the state. The price was set at 50 cents payable on Judgment Day. Nellie insisted she pay in advance and the stone was placed in 1899 by the Georgia Society of Colonial Dames.

## University of Georgia Marker
### Bay Street between Bull and Drayton Streets

In 1785 the State Legislature met in a public house between Bull and Drayton Streets owned by Thomas Stone. There, they approved legislation for the establishment of the University of Georgia, the oldest state chartered university in America. They decided to locate the campus in Athens, Georgia and the land was purchased and then donated by Savannahian John Milledge. Milledgeville was named in his honor.

## Vietnam Veterans Memorial
### Emmet Park between Habersham and Price Streets

Erected in 1990 to honor the 106 Chatham County citizens either killed or missing during the war and to the 25,000 survivors in coastal Georgia. The inscription reads, "Lest they be forgotten." The monument contains a tablet with each name listed, a pair of combat boots with an M-16 rifle bayoneted into the ground between them, and a helmet draped on the butt of the rifle. These are mounted atop a stone rendering of the country of Vietnam. A reflection pool within an iron fence surrounds the monument. The ground outside is paved with bricks bearing the names of those who assisted in financing this monument.

*Vietnam Veteran's Memorial*

## Washington Guns
### Bay Street between Bull and Drayton Streets

These cannons were presented to the Chatham Artillery by General George Washington in appreciation for services rendered during his visit to Savannah in 1791. The unit was his escort while he inspected the former British defenses of the town. General Lachlan McIntosh, one of the commanders in the battle and who was then a resident of Savannah, also accompanied Washington.

The guns were captured in the Battle of Yorktown and are dubbed affectionately, "George and Martha," probably due to their shapes. The British cannon, cast in 1758, bears the royal insignia and motto of the Order of the Garter on its barrel. It is also inscribed with the caption: "Surrendered by the capitulation of Yorktown, October, 19, 1781." The 1756 French gun bears the coat of arms of Louis XIV, the Sun King, with a Latin inscription meaning "Last Argument of Kings."

*Washington Guns*

During the Civil War, the guns were safely buried under the Chatham Artillery armory and not removed until 1872. At the centennial celebration of Cornwallis' surrender in 1881, they traveled back to Yorktown. Escorted by members of the Chatham Artillery, they led the victory parade. After the commemorative event, they returned to their permanent residence in Savannah.

## Waving Girl Memorial
### River Street and East Broad Ramp

Commemorating Florence Martus, sister of the Tybee lighthouse keeper. Florence was born on Cockspur Island in 1868 but spent most of her

*The Waving Girl*

life on Elba Island nearby. In 1887, she began waving at every ship that entered or left the port of Savannah. From the porch of her little house on Elba Island, she waved a white handkerchief by day and a lantern by night.

Many said that she waved because she hoped to be the first to greet her fiance who had gone to sea for one last voyage but had not returned. Apparently this story was no more than tourist fiction. She waved because she was friendly and lonely. It all came to an end in 1931. Her brother retired and she waved no more.

For 44 years, Florence waved at every vessel and reportedly, never missed a ship. Mail arrived from all over the world addressed to simply, "The Waving Girl." She was internationally known as sailors spread the word of Savannah's waving girl.

Florence died in 1943 and is buried in Laurel Grove Cemetery. During World War II, her name was borne by one of the liberty ships launched in Savannah.

The statue, erected in 1972, is the work of sculptor Felix de Weldon who also sculpted the Iwo Jima Monument in Washington, D.C.

## John Wesley Monument

### Reynolds Square

John Wesley was born in Lincolnshire, England at the Epworth Rectory on June 17, 1703. His father was the rector. When Oglethorpe returned to England in 1735, he asked Wesley to come to Georgia with him as the minister of Christ Church. Wesley originally declined, but under pressure from his mother, Oglethorpe, and the trustees, he finally agreed.

He and his brother Charles arrived in the colony on February 5, 1736.

Wesley was the third Anglican priest assigned to Georgia. Unfortunately, from the very beginning, there was a misunderstanding between Wesley, Oglethorpe, and the trustees. They wanted him to minister strictly to the colonists. Wesley believed he was being called to preach to the Indians, which sounded romantic and lent a sense of adventure.

The Yamacraw Indians were totally unreceptive to his preaching. He was extremely disappointed and developed a negative opinion of all Indians. Soon, he fell from grace with the settlers as well. He had been cautioned to be tolerant, but his authoritarian streak surfaced and did not sit well with the colonists. For example, he insisted on baptism by immersion unless someone was too weak to be "dipped."

The incident that proved to be his undoing was his becoming enamored with Sophey Hopkey, the niece of Thomas Causton, Oglethorpe's second in command. As the affair progressed, Wesley hesitated, being torn between his Christian mission and his feelings for Sophey.

***John Wesley Monument***

There was no question that it interfered with his ministry. Feeling spurned, she accepted a proposal from another suitor. Wesley was livid and refused to administer their marriage vows. Instead, they were married in South Carolina and upon their return, Wesley refused to give her communion. Her husband deemed this a public insult and sued Wesley for defamation of character and 1,000 pounds in damages. The warrant was served by Constable Noble Jones. Wesley insisted it was a church matter and the court had no jurisdiction. Since

Causton was also the Chief Magistrate, he set an initial court date followed by several postponements.

At last, Wesley realized the futility of his position and posted notice in Johnson Square of his intention to return to England. He left town in the dead of night in the company of a wife-beater, a bankrupt constable, and a barber. The trio fled to South Carolina and after being lost for days in the woods, finally made it to Beaufort. From there Wesley made his way to Charleston and sailed back to England.

His tenure in Georgia spanned only a year and nine months but during this brief period, he was able to start the first Protestant Sunday School and compile the first hymnal used in Georgia. For him, it was a trying period in what became an outstanding life of Christian service.

Back in England, he and his brother Charles, along with John Ingham and George Whitefield, would establish the Methodist Church at Christ Church College in Oxford. From there, Wesley became an itinerant preacher, organizing prayer societies and appointing and commissioning lay preachers. He died in 1791.

The statue depicts Wesley wearing the Church of England vestments that he wore during his Georgia ministry. His right hand is stretched forth in love while his left holds the Bible. The sculpture, by Marshall Daugherty, was dedicated in 1969.

There is also a marker on Cockspur Island at the spot where Wesley and his brother Charles first landed in Georgia. It is a short distance from Fort Pulaski.

## Wesley Services Marker

### Rear of Federal Courthouse on Wright Square

John Wesley conducted services in the little colonial courthouse from May 1736 until December 1737. It was here that he uttered his last public prayer in Georgia.

## Wesley Chapel Marker

### Lincoln Street and Oglethorpe Avenue

Savannah's first Methodist church was erected on this corner in 1812. Bishop Francis Asbury preached twice at this location. In 1848, the building became too small and the congregation erected Trinity Church on Telfair Square.

## Yellow Fever Marker
### Colonial Park Cemetery

In 1820 a ship arrived in Savannah from the West Indies with Yellow Fever on board. Within a month more than 700 were dead and the small town of 7,523 was down to 1,500 because of the panic. The spread of the disease was blamed on many causes including overpopulation, humidity, and unwholesome vapors rising from the wetlands surrounding the town. It would be another 80 years before Walter Reed identified the mosquito as the carrier of the fever.

This would not the last time for the disease that repeated until the turn of the twentieth century. In 1854, the fever returned causing more than 500 deaths. Nearly two-thirds of the city evacuated until the epidemic passed. Again in 1876 Yellow Fever struck and more than 1,000 perished.

# Buildings and Houses

## The Armstrong Mansion

**447 Bull Street**

**Bull and Gaston Streets**

***The Armstrong Mansion***

Designed by Henrik Wallin for George Ferguson Armstrong and constructed between 1916-1919 in the ***Italian Renaissance*** style. The brick was formulated from reconstructed marble dust. The house was given to the city in 1935 for what became Armstrong Atlantic State University. The college moved to the southside in 1966. The mansion is currently occupied by a law firm.

Armstrong was born in 1868 and died in 1924 and is buried in Bonaventure Cemetery. He served with the Chatham Artillery in the Spanish American War. He was recognized nationally for his ability in the shipping business.

## The Cord Asendorf House

### 1921 Bull Street
### Bull and 36th Streets

Built in 1899 by German-born grocer Cord Asendorf who came to Savannah at the age of 14. He became wealthy in mercantile and real estate and retired in his thirties. Asendorf died in 1944 and is buried in Bonaventure Cemetery. His daughter Sophie lived in the house until 1976.

*Cord Asendorff House*

Its design is known as ***"steamboat gothic"*** and the house is considered to be one of the finest examples of that style in the country. It is referred to locally as "*The Gingerbread House*" and is currently used as a reception hall.

## The Champion-McAlpin House

### 230 Barnard Street
### Orleans Square

Built in 1843 and attributed to the architect, Charles Blaney Cluskey. Cluskey's favorite form was ***Greek Revival*** and the colossal portico was copied from the Temple of the Winds in Athens, Greece.

*Champion-McAlpin House*

The original owner was bank president Aaron Champion. During the Civil War, he hid his bank's gold in the well at the rear of the house. All was recovered after the war except for a $10 dollar gold piece. Champion gave the house as a wedding gift to his daughter on her marriage to James McAlpin, son of one of the town's wealthiest citizens, Henry McAlpin. Champion died in 1880 and is buried in Laurel Grove Cemetery.

*City Hall*

His daughter and McAlpin added the top floor with the Mansard roof in 1880. The property was acquired in 1939 by preservationist Alida Harper Fowlkes. At her death in 1985, she willed it to the Society of the Cincinnati in Georgia. Fowlkes is buried in Bonaventure Cemetery.

## City Hall
### Bull and Bay Streets

Designed by Hyman Witcover in 1905. Inside, a large bronze fountain occupies the central court. The court rises to a rotunda and stained glass dome that is 30 feet wide and 70 feet high. It was from this site on the river in 1819 that the *S.S. Savannah* embarked on its voyage across the Atlantic becoming the first steamship to successfully cross any ocean.

## The Cluskey Building
### 127 Abercorn Street
### Oglethorpe Square

*The Cluskey Building*

Designed for Mary Marshall, the developer, by Charles B. Cluskey and completed in 1859. This is a good example of the style of rental property that was erected in Savannah at that time.

## The Davenport House
### 324 E. State Street
### Columbia Square

Built by Isaiah Davenport as his family home in 1820. Davenport was a master builder who was trained as a ship builder. He came to Savannah from Rhode Island in 1799 to participate in the building boom following the great fire of 1796. Davenport married Sara Clark in 1809, prospered as a master builder, served as a city alderman, and died of the Yellow Fever in 1827. The house is in ***Federal style*** with a central hall and balanced facade and interior.

*The Davenport House*

The house was scheduled for demolition in 1955 by entrepreneurs who wanted to reclaim the brick and create yet another parking lot. In opposition, a group of Savannah women, concerned about preservation, raised the necessary $22,500 to purchase the house. It was then restored and became the impetus for forming the Historic Savannah Foundation. Open to the public.

## The Eastman-Stoddard House
**233 Bull Street**
**Chippewa Square**

Began for Moses Eastman, jeweler and silversmith, in 1844 and completed for John Stoddard, a wealthy planter, in 1847. In 1893, the house was sold to Joseph Hull. The Hull family lived there until 1917 when it was purchased by Dr. Craig Barrow. The Barrows occupied the house until they moved to Wormsloe in 1939. In 1953 it was purchased by the Atlantic Mutual Fire Insurance Co. and served as their headquarters for many years. It is currently occupied by a law firm. The iron fence with its medallions of prominent men is a treasure from the Wetter House which was scheduled for demolition. The fence was moved here in 1840 from Oglethorpe Ave. and Martin Luther King, Jr., Blvd. It was originally made for the state capitol building in Milledgeville. The third story of the building was added in the twentieth century.

*Eastman-Stoddard House*

## Eppinger's Tavern
**110 E. Oglethorpe Avenue**

The oldest brick house in Georgia and thought to have been built in 1771. Initially, it operated as a tavern and inn. The building also witnessed many balls, public meetings, and religious services. After the British evacuated Savannah, it served as an early meeting place for the Georgia Legislature in what was known as Eppinger's long room. General Lachlan

*Eppinger's Tavern*

McIntosh made it his home after the Revolutionary War until his death in 1806.

## Gordon Row

### Gordon Street between Barnard and Whitaker Streets

Noted for its ironwork and interesting doorways. The row contains 15 four-story townhouses constructed in 1853 as rental property. Now it consists of privately owned residences and rental units.

*Gordon Row*

## The Green-Meldrim House

### 327 Bull Street
### Madison Square

Designed and built by John S. Norris in 1853 for Charles Green, a wealthy cotton factor, who came to Savannah from Britain in 1833 and amassed a fortune. It is one of the finest examples of domestic ***Gothic Revival*** architecture in the South. The brick exterior was originally covered with stucco. The Gothic style is repeated inside the house in both plaster and black walnut.

In 1864, after the city had surrendered to General William T. Sherman, Green offered the house to Sherman for use as his headquarters. Green's action was motivated more by his feelings of sympathy toward the people of Savannah than any loyalties to the Union. He said that maybe his action would spare some other resident of Savannah the humiliation of having Sherman occupy his home.

***Green-Meldrim House***

Green was still a British subject with southern sympathies and two sons in the army of the Confederacy. During the war, on a visit to the North, he was imprisoned for several months at Fort Warren, in Boston, because his ships were bringing in much needed medical supplies for the Confederate troops.

Savannah was spared the torch and Sherman never said why. Perhaps it was somewhat due to Savannah's hospitality. It was from this house that Sherman sent his telegram to President Lincoln presenting Savannah as a Christmas gift. Sherman remained at the house for five weeks and because Green was a British subject, he was required to pay rent. Green died in 1881 and was buried in a family plot in the Presbyterian Church Cemetery at Greenwich, Virginia.

The house was subsequently owned by Judge Peter W. Meldrim, former mayor of Savannah and once president of the American Bar Association. It was Meldrim who suggested a monument to Sergeant Jasper be erected in Madison Square. Jasper was one of the heroes of the Battle of Savannah in 1779. Meldrim then personally managed the efforts to make that monument a reality. He is buried in Bonaventure Cemetery.

In 1943 the house was purchased from the Meldrim family by St. John's Episcopal Church and is now used as its parish house. It was designated a National Historic Landmark in 1976 and is frequently open for public tours.

## The Hamilton-Turner House
### 330 Abercorn Street
### Lafayette Square

Built by J.D. Hall in 1873 for Samuel Pugh Hamilton, a jeweler and former mayor. His Great Southern Jewelry store on the corner of Whitaker and Congress Streets was reputed to be the largest jewelry store south of New York. Hamilton lived in the house until his death in 1899 and was known as the "Lord of Lafayette Square." Dr. Francis Turner purchased the house in 1918 and his family resided there until the 1960's. The house is said to be haunted by friendly ghosts. The Hamilton children were known to roll billiard balls down the stairs and similar noises have been reported by guests in recent years. The entire house is built of Savannah gray bricks covered with stucco. In all, there are five executive suites, 17 bedrooms, seven kitchens, and seven bathrooms. It is designed in the ***Second French Empire style***. The house was featured in the John Berendt book, *"Midnight in the Garden of Good and Evil."*

***The Hamilton-Turner House***

## Hodgson Hall
### 501 Whitaker Street
### Whitaker and Gaston Streets

Built in 1876 as a memorial to William Brown Hodgson, internationally known scholar and Middle East diplomat. As a dragoman (interpreter) and counsel to the Barbary states and Turkey, he was acquainted with 14 languages and spoke nine fluently. His favorite was Berber, the language of the Sahara Desert, into which he translated the Gospel according to Matthew. The funds for the building were provided by his widow, Margaret Telfair Hodgson. After her death in 1874, it was completed by her sister, Mary. It was said that both Margaret and Mary were in love with Hodgson. All three are buried in Bonaventure Cemetery in the Telfair lot.

*Hodgson Hall*

The hall designed by Detlaf Lienau, was built to house the Georgia Historical Society which began in 1839 with a charter from the state legislature. Early members included Israel K. Tefft and Alexander Smets who were both collectors. They were two of the most intellectual and cultivated men living in Savannah during the heyday of cotton, prior to the Civil War.

Smets was a Frenchman who spent a fortune on collecting rare books. His library of 5,000 books and manuscripts was among the finest anywhere. Tefft, on the other hand, was the world's greatest autograph collector. Not satisfied with merely obtaining signatures, he corresponded with the world's great leaders in virtually every field. Tefft obtained entire letters and many portrait engravings of famous people of the day. He and Smets were the closest of friends and when Smets died in May 1862, Tefft was so dejected, he died a month later. The State of Georgia was interested in acquiring Smets' collection but it was a case where no one took action. Eventually his executors took the entire collection to New York and sold it for a mere $10,000. Both Smets and Tefft are buried in Laurel Grove Cemetery.

The building houses a priceless collection of thousands of historical documents, books, pamphlets, maps, photographs, portraits, artifacts, and relics. The Historical Society is the primary source of information on the history of Savannah and Georgia. Interesting artifacts on display include General Oglethorpe's compass and snuff box, the grapeshot that killed Count Pulaski, and a drum from the Revolutionary War. A large collection of genealogical material is available for family research. The hall is open to the public.

## The Kehoe House
**123 Habersham Street**
**Columbia Square**

Built in 1893 as a single family house for William Kehoe, owner of the Kehoe Iron Works in Savannah. The house was designed by DeWitt Bruyn and is part ***Neoclassical*** and part ***Italianate***. It is currently in use as an inn.

***Kehoe House***

## Laura's Cottage
**420 E. State Street**

Built between 1799 and 1809 and named for its longtime tenant, Mrs. Laura Jones. It was moved from another location and authentically restored. The entire house is original heart pine and consists of only two rooms, the living room and dining room with a freestanding fireplace between the two.

## The Low-Colonial Dames House

**329 Abercorn Street**
**Lafayette Square**

*The Low-Colonial Dames House*

Designed by John S. Norris and built in 1848 for Andrew Low, a wealthy cotton merchant. The Victorian house combines the features of ***Italianate and Greek Revival*** design featuring elaborate brackets, iron works, silver door knobs, delicate plaster work, and high ceilings. In 1870 when Robert E. Lee visited Savannah, he was a guest of Mr. Low and a reception was held in his honor. Mr. Low died in 1886 at 73 years of age and is buried in Laurel Grove Cemetery. His son, William Mackay Low, married Juliette Gordon who founded the Girl Scouts of America while living as a widow in this house. She continued to reside here until her death in 1927.

Juliette Low bequeathed the carriage house to the Girl Scouts of Savannah. It is now used as their headquarters. The main house was purchased in 1928 by the Colonial Dames of Georgia for use as their headquarters. Juliette Low's mother, Nellie Kinzie Gordon, had been an early president of the Colonial Dames in Georgia. The house is open to the public.

## The Lucas Theatre

**Abercorn and Congress Streets**
**Reynolds Square**

Built in 1921 for theatre entrepreneur, Colonel Arthur Lucas. The large lobby and stairway leading to the mezzanine are laid in Italian marble and the ceiling has a magnificent dome which contains 620 lights. When the

Lucas opened as a vaudeville theater and cinema in 1921, it offered state of the art in patron comforts. Gentlemen were expected to wear coats and ties in the evening or be seated in the balcony. It closed as a theatre in 1976 and is now undergoing restoration to be used as a community center.

*The Lucas Theater*

## Mary Marshall Row

### Oglethorpe Avenue between Abercorn and Lincoln Streets

Mary Leaver Marshall was born in 1783, the daughter of a prosperous cabinetmaker. From him, she inherited several tracts of Savannah real estate that she was able to successfully develop. Among her projects were the Cluskey Building on Oglethorpe Square and Mary Marshall Row, consisting of four-story townhouses built in the 1850's. Another project not so well known was the old Marshall Hotel on Broughton Street between Abercorn and Drayton Streets. This hotel still exists on the second floor of this block. Most of the guest rooms are still intact. Mary Marshall died at 93 years of age and is buried in Laurel Grove Cemetery.

*Mary Marshall Row*

## Massie School
**207 E. Gordon**
**Calhoun Square**

*Massie School*

Designed by John S. Norris in the ***Greek Revival*** style and completed in 1856 as the first public school in the city. It was named in honor of Peter Massie of Glynn County, a Scottish planter who bequeathed the funds in 1841 for the erection of a school to educate the poor. During the Civil War, Union troops used it as a hospital. "The Massie Common School House" continued in use until 1974. A classroom is restored as it would have appeared in the 1850's. The school is open for tours.

## The Mercer House
**429 Bull Street**
**Monterey Square**

*The Mercer House*

Designed by John S. Norris in the ***Italianate*** style and begun in 1860 for General Hugh Weedon Mercer. Construction was abandoned at the outbreak of the Civil War when Norris returned to his home in New York. Mercer resigned his United States commission to become a brigadier general in the Confederacy. After the war, Mercer moved to Baltimore and the house was finished by Norris's assistant, DeWitt Bruyn. Mercer was the great-grandfather of songwriter Johnny Mercer and is buried in Bonaventure Cemetery. The house was featured in the John Berendt book, *Midnight in the Garden of Good and Evil.* It was in this house that the alleged murdcr, central to the story, occurred. It is a private residence.

## The Molyneaux-Jackson House
### 450 Bull Street
### Bull and Gaston Streets

Built in 1857 for Edmund Molyneaux, the British Counsel, as a ***Greek Revival*** home. Molyneaux was described by those who knew him as a bon vivant and gourmet. He returned to England in 1862 and died there in 1864. In January 1865, when Union troops occupied the city, the house was appropriated as Union headquarters by General Oliver O. Howard and his successor General William F. Barry. With their departure, many of the books from its library and all of its wine and brandy also departed.

***The Molyneaux-Jackson House***

In 1885, the house was sold to General Henry Rootes Jackson, U.S. District Attorney for Georgia. Jackson lived there until his death in 1898. Earlier in his career, he served as special prosecutor for the U.S. in the celebrated case of the slave ship, *Wanderer*, that was tried in Savannah in 1859. Jackson was an outstanding jurist, poet, Confederate brigadier general, and minister to Austria and Mexico. He was a gifted speaker and served as president of the Georgia Historical Society and a trustee of the Telfair Academy of Arts and Sciences. The best known of Jackson's poems is *"The*

*Red Old Hills of Georgia."* General Jackson is buried in Bonaventure Cemetery. The house is now occupied by the Oglethorpe Club, which is private.

***The Old Courthouse***

## The Old Courthouse

**124 Bull Street**
**Wright Square**

Designed by William G. Preston in the ***Romanesque Revival*** style and built in 1889. The building was renovated in 1990 and is now used as county offices. It was on this site that the Reverend George Whitefield preached to overflow congregations in early colonial days.

## The Oliver Sturges House

**27 Abercorn Street**
**Reynolds Square**

Built on the site of John Wesley's parsonage in Savannah. In later years Wesley said "the first rise of Methodism was in 1729 when four of us met together at Oxford. The second was in Savannah in 1736 when 20 or 30 persons met at my house."

The Sturges house is one of the twin houses of mirror image that were constructed between 1812-1813 in the ***Federal*** style. The adjacent twin was occupied by Sturges' partner, Benjamin Burroughs. It is now the site of a

***Oliver Sturges House***

hotel. The Sturges house is where the epic voyage of the *S.S. Savannah* was planned. The prime motivation behind the venture was to transport cotton quickly across the Atlantic to the British mills. Oliver Sturges was a large investor in the venture and also shipped his cotton to Liverpool via the steamship. He died in 1824, and like William Scarbrough, his partner in the *S.S. Savannah* venture, had lost most of his wealth. The house was restored in 1973 and now houses the executive offices of the Morris Newspaper Corporation.

## The Pink House
### 23 Abercorn Street
### Reynolds Square

***The Pink House***

Erected in 1789 in the ***Georgian*** style for James Habersham, Jr., son of a prominent merchant in the colony. It is one of the few buildings that survived the fire of 1796. The fanlight over the front door is one of the oldest in Georgia. Habersham died in 1799 and in 1812 it became the Planter's Bank. During the occupation of Savannah by Union troops in the Civil War, it was headquarters for the Provost Marshall's office commanded by Lt. Colonel Robert P. York.

The building became known as the "Pink House" due to the light pink shade of stucco used for the exterior. It now houses a popular restaurant.

## The Pirates' House
**20 East Broad Street**
**Trustees Garden**

Thought to have been built about 1794 when the port of Savannah was a haven for sailors from all over the world. It is said that some of the events that inspired Robert Louis Stevenson to write "*Treasure Island*" took place at this tavern. The spirit of Captain Flint allegedly roams the area called the "Captain's Room" where Flint was supposed to have died.

One of the dining rooms in the restaurant is known as the "Herb House" and may be the oldest room in Savannah. It can be identified by its walls of oversized brick painted white. Overall, the Pirates' House is a perfectly preserved seaman's tavern with a maze of rooms that seems endless.

***The Pirates House***

## The Richardson-Owens-Thomas House
**124 Abercorn Street**
**Oglethorpe Square**

The house was designed by William Jay while still in his early twenties. It was completed in 1819 for banker and cotton merchant Richard Richardson, who was related to Jay's sister. The house was built in the ***English Regency*** style and constructed with interior plumbing, which was very unusual at the time. The structure features curved walls and doors, a Jay trademark, a bridge stairway, unique crown molding throughout, and a parlor ceiling that is flat but appears rounded.

*The Richardson-Owens-Thomas House*

Richardson was president of the Savannah branch of the Second Bank of the United States. After suffering losses associated with the *S.S. Savannah* venture, his own bank had to foreclose on the house in 1822. It remained a property of the bank for eight years. During that time it served as a rooming house and accommodated many distinguished visitors including the Marquis de Lafayette who is said to have reviewed the Savannah militia units and addressed the city from the southern balcony during his visit in 1825.

The house was purchased by George Welchman Owens, past congressman and mayor, in 1830. The home stayed in his family until 1951 when his granddaughter, Miss Margaret Thomas, willed it to the Telfair Academy of Arts and Sciences. It is open to the public.

## St. Vincent's Academy
### Abercorn and Liberty Streets

Designed by Charles B. Cluskey and opened in 1845 for the Sisters of Mercy as the convent, orphanage, and academy of St. Vincent de Paul. Two of the notable students at St. Vincent's were Winnie and Jeff Davis, children of Jefferson Davis, the president of the Confederacy. Today it operates as a girl's parochial school.

## The Savannah Cotton Exchange

**100 E. Bay Street**
**Drayton and Bay Streets**

The design for this building was selected from an architectural competition won by William Gibbons Preston of Boston, a leading proponent of the ***Romanesque Revival*** style.

The city had specified that the Drayton Street ramp to the river was to be left open. This resulted in the first building in the country with "air rights" over a public street. It was erected with iron columns and granite piers for support, but with the ramp open underneath.

In front of the exchange is a terra cotta griffon, also designed by Preston, with water spewing from its mouth into an ornamental pool. A griffon is a mythological beast with the body of a lion and the wings of an eagle whose task is to guard ancient treasure. Surrounding the fountain is an elaborate ironwork railing immortalizing famous statesmen and authors in detailed medallions.

***The Savannah Cotton Exchange***

The building was completed in 1887 to house the Cotton Exchange. During this period, there were only two places in the world where the price of cotton was quoted: Liverpool and Savannah. The Cotton Exchange was chartered in 1872 to promote the interests of cotton merchants. With the new building, Factor's Walk became the Wall Street of Savannah.

Cotton production waned due to depleted soil and then ceased altogether because of the boll weevil infestation. Fortunately for the area's economy, the naval stores industry (Rosin, pitch, and turpentine) had grown substantially and by 1889, was also headquartered in the Cotton Exchange. The Exchange finally ceased operation in 1920. The building is now occupied by Solomon's Masonic Lodge Number One and is occasionally open for tours.

Solomon's Lodge was organized on February 21, 1734 and is the oldest continuously operating lodge of freemasons in the western hemisphere. It was founded by James Edward Oglethorpe and has his personal bible in safekeeping. The first nine mayors of Savannah and ten of Georgia's first 29 governors were members.

## The Savannah Theatre

**222 Bull Street**
**Chippewa Square**

Designed by William Jay in 1818 and built in only nine months. It was used as an opera house and playhouse until 1931 when it was converted into a movie theatre. It has been remodeled numerous times due to fire and obsolescence and today is in ***Art Deco*** style. It is the second oldest continuously operating theatre in America.

## The Savannah Volunteer Guards Armory

**340 Bull Street**
**Madison Square**

Designed by William G. Preston in 1892 in the ***Romanesque Revival*** style. The two cannons at the front entrance were a gift to the Guards in the late nineteenth century. The Volunteer Guards were organized in 1802. As an infantry, the corps fought in the War of 1812, Indian Wars, and as a battalion in 1861 serving with distinction in the defense of Savannah and Charleston. In the spring of 1864, the Guards joined Lee's army at Petersburg, Virginia. On April 3rd, 1865, they served in the rear guard on the Confederate retreat to Appomattox. At that time the unit had been reduced to 85 men. Of

*The Savannah Volunteer Guards Armory*

that number, 23 were killed, 35 wounded, and the remainder captured. The unit was reorganized in 1872 and served as an infantry battalion of the Spanish American War. It also served in WWI and again in WWII where it was awarded five battle stars.

The building is now used by the Savannah College of Art and Design.

## The Scarbrough House
### 41 Martin Luther King, Jr. Boulevard

Designed by William Jay in the ***Regency*** style and completed in 1819 for Julia and William Scarbrough. The house has a sweeping entry with a balcony on the second level and a high curved ceiling which makes it appear open to the sky. There are rooms on either side of the entry and a ballroom behind. The Jay trademarks are the curved walls, doors, and distinctive cornices.

*The Scarbrough House*

William Scarbrough was the son of a wealthy planter from Beaufort, South Carolina. He was educated in Europe and moved to Savannah in 1798 where he became one of the so-called merchant princes of the era. He and his wife occupied a leading place in the life of the community. She was well known for her wonderful

*William Scarbrough*

parties and they wanted a place to reflect his prosperity and provide a suitable place for her to entertain. Probably their most prominent guest was President James Monroe who came to Savannah in 1819, the year the house was completed. The reason for the visit was to see the S.S. Savannah, which Scarbrough was promoting, prior to her voyage across the Atlantic.

It is currently occupied by the Ships of the Sea Museum and is open to the public.

## The Sorrel-Weed House

### Bull and Harris Streets
### Madison Square

Completed in 1841 in the ***Greek Revival*** style for shipping merchant Francis Sorrel and attributed to the architect, Charles B. Cluskey. In his youth, it was home to G. Moxley Sorrel, one of "Lee's Lieutenants" during the Civil War. He served with the Army of Northern Virginia on General Longstreet's staff with conspicuous valor and zeal. Moxley served through their many battles from the first Battle of Bull Run to Petersburg. He was wounded three times and became a general at the age of 26. Critics have called him the best staff officer to serve in the Confederacy. He is buried in Laurel Grove Cemetery.

*The Sorrel-Weed House*

The house was purchased by Henry D. Weed in 1859 and frequented by Robert E. Lee in 1862 when he was in charge of Confederate coastal defenses. Mr. Weed is buried in Laurel Grove Cemetery. The elegant house has long been noted for the gracious hospitality of its owners and as a center of Savannah's social scene.

## The Telfair Art Museum
### 121 Barnard Street
### Telfair Square

On this site originally stood Government House, the home of the royal governors from 1760 until the end of the Revolutionary War. The present house was designed by William Jay and built for Alexander Telfair, youngest son of Governor Edward Telfair.

*The Telfair Art Museum*

Alexander operated a very successful plantation near Louisville which enabled him to build this magnificent house. He was a prominent citizen of Savannah with a keen sense of civic duty. Alexander was a founder of the Savannah Theatre and a president of the Union Society. He served as Chairman of the Board of Chatham Academy and had quite a reputation as a scholar, art patron, and lover of fine food and wine. In 1832, while in

Winchester, Virginia, Alexander contracted pleurisy which proved fatal. He was buried there at 43 years of age.

Alexander never married and at his death, the property passed to his sisters, Mary and Margaret. In 1838, they had a close call when they booked passage on the ill-fated steamer *Pulaski*. At the last minute they gave up their seats to others, and the *Pulaski* steamed north to explode and sink off the coast of Charleston.

Mary was believed to have been born about 1791. Since she was very secretive about her age, the date is not certain. She became the city's greatest benefactor during the difficult period after the Civil War. In addition to the Telfair Academy, her other public bequests include the Telfair Hospital for Females and the pulpit area of Independent Presbyterian Church. Her sister Margaret was married to William Hodgson and after his death, the sisters provided the necessary funds for the construction of Hodgson Hall that houses the Georgia Historical Society.

***Mary Telfair***

Margaret died in 1874, and Mary, a year later. Mary was an early patron of the arts and bequeathed their residence to the Georgia Historical Society. The bequest carried the provision that the house be opened to the public and be named "Telfair Academy of Arts and Sciences." Both Margaret and Mary are buried in Bonaventure Cemetery.

The mansion is representative of Jay's Regency style and was completed in 1820. The house was typical Jay features including rounded rooms, unique cornices, mantelpieces and moldings. Many of the Telfair family furnishings remain. The octagon room is one of the mansion's many attractions and was recently rediscovered and restored. The room contains the oldest known example of oak graining in the country. The process is a plaster meticulously finished to make it indistinguishable from actual wood. The mansion is one of the five designed by the young William Jay.

The Telfair opened in 1886 and is the oldest art museum in the Southeast. The expansion of the Telfair home as a museum was overseen by architect Detlef Lienau who meticulously strived to preserve Jay's classic Greek design. In front of the building are sculptures of Phidias, Michaelangelo, Raphael, Rubens, and Rembrandt. These were sculpted by Viennese sculptor V. Tilgner in 1884. The permanent collection includes paintings, sculpture, and decorative arts. Also displayed are furnishings and Savannah-made silver. Open to the public.

## The U.S. Custom House

**1 E. Bay Street**
**Bull and Bay Streets**

*The U.S. Custom House*

Designed by John S. Norris, who won an architectural competition for the building. The cornerstone was laid in 1848 and the building was completed in 1852. The structure is one of the most handsome and substantial public buildings erected during that era. It is built of granite from Quincy, Massachusetts and is notable for its six monolithic columns and their capitals showing carved tobacco leaves. Each column weighs 15 tons and was brought to Savannah aboard a sailing vessel. The building showcases an unusual double circular stairway that is attached to the wall as its only support. Each step is made of solid stone and interlocks with the next.

During the nineteenth century, federal court facilities were housed on the third floor of the building. It was in this courtroom in 1859, that the famous case of C.A.L. Lamar and the ship *"Wanderer"* was tried before

Savannah native, Justice James M. Wayne of the Supreme Court. This case involved the last violation of the law against the importation of slaves.

The site was also the location of Oglethorpe's headquarters when he was not at Frederica. It was here on March 7, 1736, that John Wesley preached his first sermon in Georgia.

## The Wayne-Gordon House
### 10 E. Oglethorpe Avenue
### Bull Street and Oglethorpe Avenue

Built in 1823 for Mayor James Moore Wayne. The architect is unknown but similarities in the ***Regency*** style suggest that William Jay may have had some involvement. The third floor and side porch were added in 1886. Wayne was appointed to the Supreme Court by President Andrew Jackson and served for 32 years. He was such a staunch unionist that he remained on the Supreme Court even after Georgia seceded from the union. His son, Henry, was a Confederate general. Wayne died in 1867 and is buried in Laurel Grove Cemetery, as is his son.

***The Wayne-Gordon House***

The house was purchased by William Washington Gordon in 1831. He was the founder and president of the Central of Georgia Railway. His wife was Wayne's niece. His granddaughter, Juliette Gordon Low, founder of the Girl Scouts of America, was born in the house in 1860. She was the daughter of William Washington Gordon II and was called "Daisy" by her family and friends. As a child Daisy sassily informed General Sherman, when his troops occupied Savannah and he came to visit, "my daddy has shot many a Yankee." Her father was a colonel in the Confederate army while her mother Nellie, had many relatives who fought for the North. In fact it was Nellie's uncle, General David Hunter, who was in charge of Union forces during their attack on Fort Pulaski in Savannah.

*Juliette Gordon Low*

Daisy was educated in some of the finest northern boarding schools and grew up to be an eccentric, even wearing live vegetables on her hat and going trout fishing with Rudyard Kipling in full evening dress. She was raised with many advantages by her wealthy parents and traveled extensively throughout the United States and Europe. Life was enjoyed to the hilt as she hobnobbed with influential relatives and family friends.

She was practically deaf in one ear after insisting that her doctor treat an earache with silver nitrate. Then, at her wedding in 1886, a grain of rice lodged in her good ear and left her deaf in that ear as well. She was unhappily married to William Mackay Low, a British cotton broker in Savannah. Daisy called him "Billow." While married, she met many of the British upper-crust and led a life of ease and affluence. Billow deserted her for another woman and she was on the brink of filing for divorce when he died. Most of his estate was left to his mistress.

After becoming a widow, Daisy wandered aimlessly between Savannah, England, and Scotland. At the age of 50, she met General Robert Baden-Powell who was a British military hero and organizer of the Boy Scouts in England. His sister, Agnes, had organized a similar group for girls called the Girl Guides. This gave Daisy the idea of starting a comparable program for girls in America.

On March 12, 1912 she formed the first two patrols of the Girl Guides, later the Girl Scouts, beginning a movement affecting the lives of more than 50 million women. In her final years, she was usually seen in her Girl Scout uniform with a campaign hat on her head and a whistle and tin cup at her waist. She died of cancer in 1927 and is buried in her Girl Scout uniform in the family lot in Laurel Grove Cemetery.

In 1953, the Girl Scouts purchased the house and today it operates as a house museum. It was named Savannah's first National Historic Landmark in 1965.

# Architects and Styles

## Charles Blaney Cluskey

Cluskey came to Savannah from Ireland, probably as early as 1829. During his stay he left his imprint on the town by designing the ***Champion-McAlpin House,*** the ***Cluskey Building,*** the ***Eastman-Stoddard House, Mary Marshall Row, St. Vincent's Academy,*** the ***Sorrel-Weed House,*** and ***Stoddard's Range*** on Factor's Walk.

## William Jay

Jay was only 24years of age when he came to Savannah from Bath, England in 1817. He was one of the few professional architects working in America. In Savannah he found a wealthy clientele and no competition. His first design was a house for Richard Richardson, president of the Savannah branch of the Second Bank of the United States and an in-law of his sister Anne. It is now know as the ***Richardson-Owens-Thomas House,*** built in the English Regency style. The ***Scarbrough House*** is also a Jay creation. Others were the ***Savannah Theatre,*** the ***Telfair House*** (now the Telfair Art Museum), and possibly the ***Wayne-Gordon House***. Two of Jay's creations that fell victim to the wrecking ball were the ***Savannah branch of the Second Bank of the United States*** and the ***Bulloch-Habersham House.***

In 1820, Savannah was caught in the throes of a national economic depression while suffering a large fire plus a Yellow Fever epidemic. At that point Jay moved to Charleston where he only lived for a short period before returning to England. After a period of intense creative activity, he accepted a government appointment to the island of Mauritius in the Indian Ocean. Jay died there of fever at the age of 32.

## John S. Norris

Norris appeared on the Savannah scene in 1846 as the architect for the ***U.S. Custom House***. He also designed the ***Green-Meldrim House,*** the ***Low-Colonial Dames House, Massie School,,*** the ***Mercer House,*** the ***Unitarian Universalist Church,*** the ***Abrahams Home*** on Broughton Street at East Broad, and the ***Rogers Houses*** on Monterey Square.

### William Gibbons Preston

Preston's vehicle of expression was the Romanesque Revival style. His rendering was the winner of the competition for the design of the ***Savannah Cotton Exchange***. While in Savannah, he also designed the ***Old Courthouse Building*** on Wright Square and the ***Savannah Volunteer Guards Armory*** on Madison Square. He was instrumental in the rebuilding of Independent Presbyterian Church, using its former design, after the downtown fire of 1889. Preston designed two prominent residences in Savannah: the ***Baldwin house*** at 225 E. Hall Street and the ***William Hardee House*** at 223 E. Gwinnett Street.

## Architectural Styles

### Federal

This style is based on the work of Scottish architect Robert Adam who was prominent in England in the 1760's and 1770's. The exterior is usually elegant but rectangular or square. Look for elliptical fan-shaped windows over the front door, slender curved iron stair railings, and Palladian or Venetian windows. The style may display stone lintels over windows, a belt course between floors, and arched windows in dormers. The best examples are the ***Davenport House*** and the ***Oliver Sturges House.***

### Georgian

The Georgian style was developed in England by Inigo Jones, Christopher Wren, and James Gibbs. It was based on the Italian Renaissance vision of order, balance, and dignity. Structures are built with a symmetrical formal boxlike facade with a hipped roof. Chimneys are on the end and sometimes quoins are used to highlight the corners. The style may contain a Palladian central window and keystone lintels accompanied by sash windows with heavy dividers, or "muntins." Savannah's best known Georgian architecture is displayed by the ***Pink House***.

## Gothic Revival

Gothic Revival is known for richly carved details on pinnacles and chimneys and usually big entry halls. The style is skyward reaching and was used on many churches of the period. Examples are the ***Beth Eden Baptist Church, Cathedral of St. John the Baptist, Green-Meldrim House, Lutheran Church of the Ascension, St. Johns Episcopal Church, Temple Mickve Israel, Unitarian Universalist Church,*** *and* ***Wesley Monumental United Methodist Church***.

## Greek Revival

Buildings are identified by a gabled portico or temple facade of one or two stories with columns of the Greek Doric or Ionic orders. Sometimes apparent are columns in relief on the wall, or pilasters. Roof slopes are low and may be hidden behind parapets and heavy cornices. The construction is post and beam. Examples are the ***Champion-McAlpin House, Christ Episcopal Church, First Baptist Church, First Bryan Baptist Church, Massie School,*** and ***Trinity United Methodist Church.***

## Italianate

The Italianate style was inspired by rambling northern Italian farmhouses. Typical features include square bays, a low gabled roof with wide overhanging eaves supported by large decorative brackets, a campanile-like entrance tower, and roundheaded windows with hood, or "eyebrow" moldings. Buildings may also have a cast-iron front with an elaborate entrance. Examples are the ***Kehoe House***, the ***Low-Colonial Dames House***, and the ***Mercer House.***

## Regency

The most ardent practitioner in Savannah was William Jay. Examples are the ***Richardson-Owens-Thomas House,*** the ***Scarbrough House***, the ***Telfair Art Museum***, and the ***Wayne-Gordon House.***

### Romanesque Revival

Evidenced in Savannah primarily by the work of William G. Preston. Characterized by arch and dome construction. Look for Corinthian column capitals, roof balustrades, a dome, and classical pediment or portico. Examples are the ***Old Courthouse, the Savannah Cotton Exchange,*** and the ***Savannah Volunteer Guards Armory***.

### Second French Empire

The name is a reference to Napoleon III's extensions at the Louvre in Paris. It emphasizes picturesque vertical accents on tops of buildings, such as corner pinnacles or chimneys. Also featured are turrets and domes reminiscent of French Renaissance architecture in the seventeenth century.

Second Empire has been described as a somewhat impure and ornate version of palatial architecture. It reflects a smattering of the Picturesque and French Renaissance in the use of towers and mansard roofs. Savannah's prime example is the ***Hamilton-Turner House***.

## Prominent in Savannah

### Azaleas

The azalea is a type of rhododendron. The variety most often seen in Savannah bears large trumpet shaped flowers in brilliant reds, pinks, and whites. It has a blooming season of about eight weeks during March and April.

### Ornamental Ironwork

Ornamental ironwork was a latecomer to Savannah. Only after the Great Fire of 1796 was there a concern for durability and thus a demand for iron railings and gates. Most was supplied by the foundries of Henry McAlpin at the Hermitage Plantation on the Savannah River, the Rose brothers in their Indian Street Foundry, Rourke Ironworks, or the Kehoe Foundry on East Broughton Street, which is still standing.

***Iron Walkway over Abercorn Street Ramp to River Street***

Many of the same scrolled designs appear around the monuments and fountains in the squares as well as on the buildings that face them. The same styled balconies can be seen suspended from Greek Revival mansions, Romanesque commercial buildings, and Gothic homes. The spire of the Independent Presbyterian Church is of iron as is the Old Harbor Light that guides ships into port.

## Spanish Moss

The plant is a bromeliad and a member of the pineapple family. It is not a parasite and does not choke the tree as many believe. It is a perching plant that draws nourishment from the leaf mold and other debris which collects on the tree. There is no harm to the tree other than slightly reducing the amount of sunlight it receives. The moss moves about by simply letting go and floating off in a breeze.

In the late 19th century it was boiled in chemicals and used to stuff mattresses and furniture. Normally, it is a haven for chiggers (red bugs) and visitors would be wise to leave it on the trees.

***Spanish Moss in Crepe Myrtle on East Bolton Street***

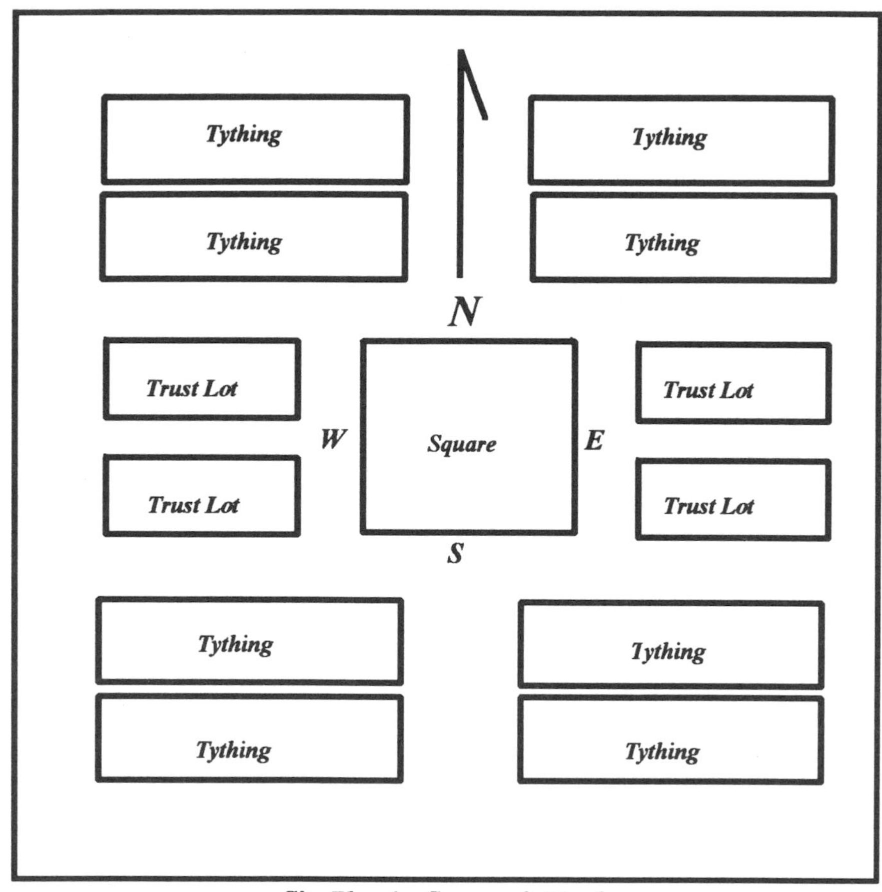


*Site Plan for Savannah Wards*

The diagram depicts the layout of a typical ward in Savannah with the square being the central point. A ward contains four trust lots, two on each side of the square, east and west. These were initially intended for public buildings and churches. Around each square are four tythings, two on the north and two on the south with a lane dividing each into two parts. These were for the colonists' private homes. The word "tything" means ten, corresponding to the number of lots each contains, with five being positioned on each block. Most tything lots measure 60 x 90 feet.

No square has the same name as the monument in the center. This isn't so strange when you realize the squares were laid out and named long before their monuments were placed. Many were named to honor military heroes or victories. Some were even renamed to honor a prominent citizen or event. The town was initially planned by Oglethorpe with four squares and eventually expanded to 24. Savannah has managed to retain 22 of these still in active use. Unfortunately, both Elbert and Liberty Squares on Montgomery Street were erased to provide unbroken access for U.S. Highway 17 that ran through Savannah.

Many monuments were erected in the Victorian period, about 1875 to 1910, when it was fashionable to honor early heroes. It has long been the custom that statues of military heroes face the enemy. For example, Oglethorpe's statue in Chippewa Square faces south against the Spanish in Florida, whereas the statue of the Confederate soldier in Forsyth Park faces north.

It is said the squares in Savannah have controlled urban expansion without allowing a formless sprawl. Or, in the vernacular of land planners, "they have provided a wonderful sense of space in a solidly built townscape." Others more to the point have said, "the squares are the jewels of Savannah, guard them well."

The presentation here is first the squares, north to south, beginning on the western side of town. It will be helpful to refer to the map of the downtown area. The parks are discussed separately.

## Montgomery Street

### Franklin Square
**Montgomery and St. Julian Streets**

Laid out in 1791 and named for Benjamin Franklin, the colony's agent in London from 1768 to 1775. Franklin corresponded with Noble Jones and even sent samples of Chinese rice to Savannah to promote the area's rice culture. For many years the square was the site of the city's water tower and was referred to as "Water Tower Square."

**Located on the square:** First African Baptist Church and the western end of the City Market area.

*The old water tower in Franklin Square*

## Liberty Square
### Montgomery and President Streets

Laid out in 1799 and named to perpetuate the dawn of freedom and independence and to honor the Savannah patriots, "The Liberty Boys". This group was instrumental in stoking the fires of the American Revolution in Georgia. The square was cleared to route U.S. Highway 17 through Savannah in 1928 and convert Montgomery Street into a thoroughfare. It also accommodated the new courthouse when it was erected.
**Monument:** the Flame of Freedom in front of the courthouse.

## Elbert Square
### Montgomery and McDonough Streets

Laid out in 1801 and named for Samuel Elbert, statesman and hero of the Revolutionary War. Elbert was born in Prince William Parish in North Carolina in 1740. Losing his parents early, he moved to Savannah and became a successful merchant and Indian trader, attaining a position of influence in the town. Elbert was an active member of the Liberty Boys, the first Council of Safety, and a delegate to the Georgia Provincial Congress. Prior to the Revolution, he served as captain of a grenadier company and later as a colonel in the Continental Army.

When General McIntosh left Georgia to join George Washington in Valley Forge, Elbert was promoted to Commander of Continental Forces in Georgia. In 1778, during the British attack on Savannah, he realized that Girdardeau's Bluff (President Street Extension across from Savannah Golf Club) was the key to defending the town. Elbert urged General Howe to occupy it in force but Howe refused. His refusal proved to be a fatal error and the primary cause of defeat resulting in Savannah's capture by the British. Elbert gallantly commanded the Georgia troops during this battle. He was taken prisoner at Briar Creek in 1779 but exchanged in 1781. Immediately, he re-established himself in the army and was in command of a brigade during the siege of Yorktown.

***Samuel Elbert***

In 1785, after the war, Elbert was elected governor. He also served as sheriff of Chatham County and Grandmaster of the Georgia Masons. Elbert died in Savannah in 1788 and is buried in Colonial Park Cemetery. Elbert County was named in his honor. Only the western portion of the square remains. The eastern half was removed in order to convert Montgomery Street into a thoroughfare.

# Barnard Street

## Ellis Square
### Barnard and St. Julian Streets

Laid out in 1733 and named for Henry Ellis, the second Royal Governor. Although he lived in Government House on Telfair Square, this square was on the path of his daily walk through the town. Ellis was extremely diplomatic, doing much to undo the ill will stirred up by his predecessor, John Reynolds. He arrived in 1757 and immediately identified three primary problems of the colony: weak defenses, small population, and a meager public treasury.

Ellis went about strengthening the fortifications by building stockades at strategic points. To increase the population, he passed a law promising protection for any debtor that could cross the Savannah River into Georgia without being caught. This, of course, did not apply to South Carolinians. He was able to increase public finances by doubling the tax on land and slaves.

One of his most important enactments proved to be the establishment of the Church of England in Georgia. This divided the colony into eight parishes. Ellis was a consummate politician, an able diplomat with the Creek Indians, and a very popular governor with the colonists. Through his efforts, the long standing claims of Mary Musgrove for Indian land were settled.

Ellis was a confirmed bachelor and generous host who loved to entertain. He was renowned for the great variety of delicacies that were served from his table. At his own request, he was relieved as governor in 1760.

The square was often referred to as "Market Square" as it was the site of markets, even from early days. It was here that the "Old City Market" was located. For many years it was a landmark, but was destroyed in 1953 to make way for the parking garage that occupies the square today.
**Located on the square:** the eastern end of the City Market area.

## Telfair Square
### Barnard and President Streets

Laid out in 1733 as St. James Square and named for the royal residence in London. It was renamed in 1883 to honor Edward Telfair, a three-time governor of Georgia and his daughter, Mary who lived on the square for many years.

Telfair was born in 1735 in Town Head, Scotland. He arrived in Georgia in 1766. Before long he joined the Liberty Boys in their rising discontent against England and became one of their most prominent rebels. Telfair was active in the secret meetings at Tondee's Tavern, raising donations for the city of Boston during their embargo resulting from the "Boston Tea Party," and leading the raid that broke open the royal powder magazine.

He served as a member of the Continental Congress from 1777-1783 and three times as governor of Georgia, 1786, 1789, and 1792. His primary business was shipbuilding but he also accumulated large holdings of land, especially after the Revolution. So successful were his businesses that at his death in 1807, he left a huge fortune. Telfair County was named in his honor. He is buried in Bonaventure Cemetery.

The square was also home to George Walton, one of the signers of the Declaration of Independence. His house was on the northwest corner. That corner later gained notoriety as Brown's Inn and Tavern, where George Washington stayed during his visit to the city in 1791. Lachlan McIntosh lived on the square but left the city after his duel with Button Gwinnett. The McIntosh house was used as a court during British occupation. The square was also the home of Joseph Gibbons whose granddaughter, Sarah, married Edward Telfair.

**Located on the square:** Telfair Art Museum and Trinity United Methodist Church.

## Orleans Square
### Barnard and McDonough Streets

Laid out in 1815 and named to honor the American victory at the Battle of New Orleans. This was the last battle of the War of 1812 with the British. The irony was that it took place 15 days after the peace treaty had been signed in Belgium. Slow communications prevented the armies from receiving word in time.

It was at a public auction in this square in 1815 that Henry McAlpin purchased the Hermitage Plantation. McAlpin was a Scottish citizen who could not legally purchase land and employed an agent to secretly represent him. McAlpin built an iron foundry along with brick ovens on the plantation and supplied much of the material for constructing the historic homes that are so admired today.

**Located on the square:** the Champion-McAlpin House.

**Monument:** the German Memorial Fountain.

*Henry McAlpin*

## Pulaski Square
### Barnard and Macon Streets

Laid out in 1837 and named in honor of Polish Count Casimir Pulaski, the highest ranking foreign officer to die in the American Revolution. Pulaski received a mortal wound in the Battle of Savannah in 1779.

**Located on the square:** the house of Confederate hero Francis S. Bartow stands on the northeast corner of the square.

*William Pitt*

## Chatham Square
### Barnard and Wayne Streets

Laid out in 1847 and named for William Pitt, the Earl of Chatham, an early friend to the colony. The name honors not only the man, but his ideals as well. Prior to the American Revolution, Pitt protested the British policy of taxation on the colonies in the House of Lords. He was adamant about the British obligation to support its subjects wherever they lived and

whatever the circumstances. His speeches were so powerful and eloquent that law students would say to each other, "Don't miss Parliament, Old Pitt is speaking." He was later elected Prime Minister of England. Although Pitt was never in Savannah, Chatham County and Chatham Square were named in his honor.
**Located on the square:** Gordon Row, consisting of 15 four-storied townhouses. Each is 20-feet wide and of identical architecture.

## Bull Street

The squares along the Bull Street promenade are those with major monuments or statues. With the exception of the Gordon Monument in Wright Square, it is the street of military heroes. Bull Street is also the street that divides the city into east and west.

### Johnson Square
**Bull and St. Julian Streets**

Laid out in 1733 and named for Robert Johnson, the Royal Governor of South Carolina when Georgia was founded. It was Savannah's first square and the site of the trustees' public store along with the mill and oven where the colonists obtained their bread. Johnson Square has always been thought of as the commercial hub in Savannah. The Declaration of Independence was read here on August 10, 1776, and in 1819 it was the site of a reception for President James Monroe. Eminent men who have spoken here include the Marquis de Lafayette in 1825, Henry Clay in 1847, and Daniel Webster in 1848.
**Located on the square:** Christ Episcopal Church.
**Monuments:** General Nathanael Greene, George

*Johnson Square Fountain*

Washington's second in command during the Revolutionary War. Greene's remains are buried here along with those of his son. The William Bull Sundial, dedicated to the man who surveyed and laid out the town for Oglethorpe. There are twin fountains located on the east and west sides.

## Wright Square
### Bull and President Streets

Laid out in 1733 and originally named Percival Square in honor of Viscount Percival, the Lord of Egmont. Percival was president of the Georgia trustees. The square was renamed in 1763 to honor Georgia's last Royal Governor, James Wright.

Wright was born in South Carolina in 1716 and served as attorney general of that state for 20 years. In 1757, he was appointed South Carolina's agent, representing them in London. While there, in 1760, he was appointed Royal Governor of Georgia, succeeding Henry Ellis.

Wright possessed a great deal of common sense, realizing his mission was not only to enforce the commands of Parliament and collect the king's revenues, but also to advance the interests of the people he governed. Wright did all he could to attract new settlers, mainly small farmers, who would protect the frontier. When South Carolina attempted to annex the area between the Altamaha and St. Mary's Rivers in 1763, Wright blocked the attempt.

*James Wright*

During a trip to England in 1772, he was knighted by the king. The following year he returned to Savannah and was met by an admiring and welcoming populace.

As busy as he was, he was still able to accumulate substantial property. By 1775 he was one of the largest planters in the colony owning eleven plantations with 25,578 acres and 523 slaves.

At a time when other colonial governors were in fear of their lives, Wright continued to enjoy the respect and affection of the people. As rebellion toward England grew, he continued his appeal to the people for loyalty and to the Crown for understanding and leniency toward the colonists. However, as the king's representative in Georgia, he believed it his duty to carry out his orders, even when he did not agree with them.

After open rebellion occurred, he was placed under house arrest, but was able to escape and flee to England. In 1779, after the British capture of Savannah, he was ordered back to Georgia to reinstate royal government. Georgia was the only colony where Crown rule was reenacted. Wright returned to Georgia but his office carried not even the shadow of authority. It was with sadness and probably relief that he left Savannah for the final time when British forces withdrew in 1782. Wright died in 1785 and is buried in Westminster Abbey in London.

The square was commonly called "Courthouse Square" since even from early days, there was a courthouse.

**Located on the square:** Lutheran Church of the Ascension and the Old Courthouse.

**Monuments:** William Washington Gordon, founder of the Central of Georgia Railroad. Also, Tomochichi, Mico (Chief) of the Yamacraw Indians.

## Chippewa Square
### Bull and McDonough Streets

Laid out in 1815 and named for the Battle of Chippewa in the War of 1812.

**Located on the square:** First Baptist Church, the Savannah Theatre, and the Eastman-Stoddard House. On the north end of the square, facing Hull Street, is the location for the bench in the movie, "*Forrest Gump.*"

**Monument:** James Edward Oglethorpe, the colony's founder.

## Madison Square
### Bull and Macon Streets

Laid out in 1837 and named to honor James Madison, the country's fourth president.

**Located on the square:** St. John's Episcopal Church, the Green-Meldrim House, the Sorrel-Weed House, and the Savannah Volunteer Guards Armory.
**Monuments:** Sergeant William Jasper, who was killed in the Battle of Savannah in 1779. A marker designating the southern line of British defense during the 1779 siege of Savannah. Cannons commemorating Georgia's first two highways: the Ogeechee Road (originally the Darien Road, laid out in 1735 with the assistance of Tomochichi) and the Augusta Road.

### Monterey Square
#### Bull and Wayne Streets

Laid out in 1847 to memorialize the 1846 capture of Monterey, Mexico by General Zachary Taylor's American forces. This was a battle of the Mexican War in which a local militia unit, the Irish Jasper Greens, fought.
**Located on the square:** Temple Mickve Israel, the Mercer House, and the Rogers Houses on the northwest trust lot.
**Monument:** Polish Count Casimir Pulaski, who gave his life for the American cause and died in the Battle of Savannah in 1779.

## Abercorn Street

### Reynolds Square
#### Abercorn and St. Julian Streets

*Rogers Houses on Monterey Square*

Laid out in 1733 and later named for Georgia's first Royal Governor, John Reynolds. It was the site of his first governmental meetings. Unfortunately, after Reynolds arrived in 1754, he mangled the affairs of Georgia so badly that he was recalled three years after his appointment. Reynolds was a seaman who had more experience giving orders on a ship than handling a provincial government. He disregarded the law and even had one man hung two days before his appointed execution. To cover his illegal acts, he resorted to altering the legislative minutes. When he was unable to force his will on the assembly, he dissolved it.

The square was the location of the Filature House, the focus of silk industry hopes in Savannah. The house was also used for government meetings and public gatherings until its destruction by fire in 1839. When George Washington visited Savannah in 1791, the Filature House was the site of the grand ball.

*Lafayette Square Fountain*

**Located on the square:** the Pink House, the Oliver Sturges House, and the Lucas Theatre.
**Monument:** John Wesley, the founder of Methodism. This square was the site of John Wesley's parsonage (where the Oliver Sturges House stands today) when he was Anglican minister to the colony in 1736.

## Oglethorpe Square
### Abercorn and President Streets

Laid out in 1742 in honor of James Edward Oglethorpe, the founder of Georgia. (See Oglethorpe Monument in "Monuments and Markers" for expanded details on James Oglethorpe.)
**Located on the square:** the Richardson-Owens-Thomas House and the Cluskey Building.
**Monument:** the Moravian Marker

## Lafayette Square
### Abercorn and Macon Streets

Laid out in 1837 and named in honor of the Marquis de Lafayette.

(See Lafayette's visit in 1825 in "Events" for expanded details on the Marquis de Lafayette.)
**Located on the square:** the Low-Colonial Dames House, the Hamilton-Turner House, and the Cathedral of St. John the Baptist. Near the southeast corner of the square is the house where Flannery O'Conner, the writer, spent her childhood. On the southeast corner is the former home of John B. Gallie, the commander of Fort McAllister, who was killed in one of several assaults by Union gunboats.
**Monument:** a fountain in the center of the square, donated by the Colonial Dames of America.

### Calhoun Square
#### Abercorn and Wayne Streets

Laid out in 1851 and named in honor of John C. Calhoun of South Carolina, the fiery politician who championed states' rights prior to the Civil War. Calhoun served as U.S. Senator from South Carolina and also as Vice President under both John Quincy Adams and Andrew Jackson.. In 1819, while serving as Secretary of War under James Monroe, he visited Savannah.

*John C. Calhoun*

This is the only square in the city that is still intact with all of the historic buildings preserved.
**Located on the square:** Massie School and Wesley Monumental United Methodist Church.

## Habersham Street

### Warren Square
#### Habersham and St. Julian Streets

Laid out in 1791 and named in honor of General Joseph Warren who was killed at the Battle of Bunker Hill during the Revolutionary War. Warren was a Massachusetts resident and an active protester against British laws. He served as president of the Massachusetts Provincial Assembly and commanded the Massachusetts forces as a major general.. The square has received much preservation attention in recent years with many of the houses being restored.

## Columbia Square
### Habersham and President Streets

Laid out in 1799 and named "Columbia," the female personification of the United States of America.

**Located on the square:** the Davenport House and the Kehoe House.

**Monument:** a fountain brought from Wormsloe Plantation in 1970 and dedicated to the memory of Augusta and Wymberley DeRenne. The DeRennes were one of Savannah's most distinguished families, being descendants of Noble Jones, an original settler.

*DeRenne Fountain*

*George Michael Troup*

## Troup Square
### Habersham and McDonough Streets

Laid out in 1851 and named in honor of George Michael Troup, Congressman, U.S. Senator and Governor of Georgia from 1823 to 1827. Troup was a leading spokesman

for states' rights and the southern cause.
**Located on the square:** the Unitarian Universalist Church and McDonough Row Houses.
**Monument:** Armillary Sphere, placed in the square in the 1970's. The sphere is an astronomical device designed after those of ancient origin and used to demonstrate relationships among the celestial circles.

## Whitefield Square
### Habersham and Wayne Streets

***George Whitefield***

Laid out in 1851, Whitefield was the last of the city squares. It was named in honor of the Reverend George Whitefield, the fourth minister to the colony and the founder of Bethesda Orphanage. He was born in Gloucester, England in 1714.

The idea for the home was conceived by Charles Wesley and supported by James Oglethorpe. In 1737, accompanied by James Habersham, Whitefield embarked for Georgia on the *Whitaker*, a transport ship carrying troops to the colony. Rather than receiving his salary as minister of Christ Church, he accepted a grant from the trustees to begin the orphanage. Until Bethesda was built, Whitefield rented a large house in Savannah and took in as many orphans as he could accommodate. The statue to this great evangelist is not in any

***Gazebo in Whitefield Square***

Savannah square, but in Philadelphia. There, at the University of Pennsylvania, resides an eight-foot bronze statue of Whitefield. Lord Chesterfield called him the "greatest orator I ever heard. I cannot conceive of a greater." Whitefield died in 1770 on a trip to Newburyport, Massachusetts, and was entombed there. His remains were placed in a coffin with a removal lid. For years, the devout came to visit his shrine and would open the coffin and feel his bones for inspiration. The vault was sealed in 1932. Whitefield County was named in his honor.

**Located on the square:** First Congregational Church

**Monument:** a gazebo in keeping with the architecture of the area where Victorian wooden houses dominate. The gazebo has been the site of many outdoor weddings.

## Houston Street

***Seamen's House on Washington Square***

### Washington Square
#### Houston and St. Julian Streets

Laid out in 1791 and named in honor of George Washington, the first President of the United States.

**Located on the square:** some of the oldest houses in the city.

### Greene Square
#### Houston and President Streets

Laid out in 1799 to honor General Nathanael Greene, Revolutionary War hero. (See Nathanael Greene Monument in "Monuments and Markers" for expanded details on Nathanael Greene.)
**Located on the square:** Second African Baptist Church.

### Crawford Square
#### Houston and McDonough Streets

Laid out in 1841 to honor William Harris Crawford, a Georgia native. Crawford was President James Madison's Secretary of the Treasury and later Minister to France during the reign of Napoleon. He was said to be the only foreign envoy with any influence over Napoleon. Many considered him to be the most respected man in America. Most political observers felt that Crawford would succeed Madison as president. Madison however, asked him to step aside and support the candidacy of James Monroe. Crawford agreed.

The Monroe Doctrine was drafted in Crawford's Georgia home. After Monroe's election, Crawford suffered an illness that left him partially paralyzed. The paralysis damaged his public image as a strong candidate in the 1824 election. Actually, no candidate received a majority and the election was thrown into the House of Representatives. They chose John Quincy Adams as president. Crawford retired from national politics and became a circuit judge in Georgia until his death in 1834. Crawford County was named in his honor.

## Parks

### Emmet Park
#### Bay Street between Abercorn and East Broad Streets

The park was named at the request of the Irish citizens who lived in the area. They wished to honor the Irish patriot and orator, Robert Emmet.

Emmet actively solicited both Napoleon and Tallyrand of France to support Irish independence from Britain. The event that led to his demise was his inciting his followers in Dublin to an uprising, then attempting to capture the Viceroy. Unfortunately, two people were killed. Emmet was arrested and convicted by a special court, then hanged by the British in 1803. He was only 25 years of age.

The park was once an Indian burial ground referred to as Indian Hill. The eastern end is where the gunpowder was stored that was stolen by the Liberty Boys prior to the Revolutionary War. Much of it was sent north and used in the Battle of Bunker Hill.
**Located on the park:** sections of Factor's Walk.
**Monuments:** the Georgia Hussars Marker, the Salzburger Monument, the Celtic Cross, the Vietnam Memorial, the Chatham Artillery Memorial, and the Old Harbor Light.

## Forsyth Park
### Bull and Gaston Streets

This is a 30-acre park bounded by Gaston Street on the north, Park Avenue on the south, Drayton Street on the east and Whitaker Street on the west. The perimeter around the park is one mile and 46 feet.

The northern section of the park was originally set aside by William Hodgson, a private citizen, who felt the city needed a large park. It was referred to as Hodgson Park. In 1851, the park was expanded to its present size and named for John Forsyth, a Georgia governor. The name had been magnanimously suggested by William Hodgson.

Forsyth was born in 1780 in Fredericksburg, Virginia and educated at Princeton. He was appointed attorney general of Georgia in 1808. During his colorful career, he served as congressman, U.S. senator, governor of Georgia, minister to Spain, and secretary of state under both Andrew Jackson and Martin Van Buren. Forsyth was known for his polish and tact. As an orator, he was said to have few equals and was considered to be the most powerful debater of his time. He died in 1841 and is buried in the Congressional Cemetery in Washington, D.C.
**Located on the park:** the Armstrong Mansion, the Molyneaux-Jackson House, and Hodgson Hall.
**Monuments:** the Forsyth Fountain, the Confederate Monument including

busts of Francis Bartow and Lafayette McLaws, the Marine Corps Monument, and the Spanish-American War Monument
**Buildings:** there are two "dummy forts" that are located in the central section of the park, one on the east and the other on the west. They were constructed about 1909 to be used as training forts for military exercises. This seemed appropriate since the south end of the park had traditionally been used as a drilling and parade ground for many militia groups in the city. In 1963, the western fort was converted to the Fragrant Garden for the Blind. The eastern fort is used as a storage shed for the city's cultural affairs program.

## Morrell Park
### River Street at East Broad Ramp

The park was named after William G. Morrell, who headed the Park and Tree Commission for many years.
**Monuments:** the Waving Girl, the Olympic Flame, and the ship *Liberty* Marker.

## Rousakis Riverfront Plaza
### River Street at Abercorn Ramp

Landscaped in the 1970's and named for Savannah's longtime mayor, John P. Rousakis.
**Located on River Street:** the river view of the commercial warehouses used in the cotton and rice trade. These have now been converted into shops and restaurants.
**Monuments:** the Merchant Marine Memorial

## Streets

*Northwest corner of Jones and Lincoln Streets*

**Abercorn Street** - named for the Right Honorable James, Earl of Abercorn, an early benefactor of the colony.

**Anderson Street** - named for Edward C. Anderson, mayor 1854-56, 1865-69, and 1873-77.

**Barnard Street** - named for Sir John Barnard, merchant, statesman, member of Parliament, and generous contributor to the trustees' fund.

**Bay Street** - in the days of the colony it was known as "the Strand." After the Revolutionary War, this name was too British for the citizens and the name was changed to "Bay Street" for its proximity to the river.

**Berrien Street** - named for Savannahian John MacPherson Berrien, U.S. Senator and attorney general under President Andrew Jackson.

**Bolton Street** - named for John Bolton, early merchant and alderman and first Postmaster of Savannah.

**Bryan Street** - named for Jonathan Bryan who aided William Bull and James Oglethorpe in laying out the town site, providing labor, and dealing with the Indians.

**Broughton Street** - named for Thomas Broughton who was Lt. Governor of South Carolina when the colony was founded. He became governor of South Carolina when Robert Johnson died in 1735.

**Bull Street** - named for William Bull who surveyed the area for the town.

**Burroughs** - named for Henry K. Burroughs, mayor from 1845-48.

**Canal Street** - named for its proximity to the Savannah and Ogeechee Canal.

**Charlton Street** - named for Thomas U.P. Charlton, alderman and six term mayor who served during the fire and Yellow Fever epidemic of 1820. He is buried in Laurel Grove Cemetery.

**Congress Street** - formerly Duke Street. Name changed in 1803 after the Revolutionary War to show a freedom from royalty.

**Drayton Street** - named for Anne and Thomas Drayton, a South Carolina couple, who loaned four sawyers to construct the original buildings.

**East Broad Street** - formerly East Boundary, the eastern boundary of the original townsite.

**Fahm Street** - named for Frederick Fahm, a large property owner on the westside of town.

**Gaston Street** - named for William Gaston, Savannah's legendary host and philanthropist.

**General McIntosh Boulevard** - named for General Lachlan McIntosh, hero of the Revolutionary War and prominent Savannah citizen.

**Gordon Street** - named for William Washington Gordon, developer of the Central of Georgia Railroad and a mayor of Savannah.

**Greene Street** - named for General Nathanael Greene, hero of the Revolutionary War.

**Gwinnett Street** - named for Button Gwinnett, signer of the Declaration of Independence from Georgia.

**Habersham Street** - named for James Habersham, who assisted George Whitefield in establishing Bethesda Orphanage and held many offices in the early years of the province.

**Hall Street** - named for Dr. Lyman Hall, signer of the Declaration of Independence from Georgia.

**Harris Street** - named for Charles Harris, mayor and long time alderman in the late 1800's.

**Henry Street** - named for Jacob P. Henry, prominent businessman and alderman 1816-1828.

**Houston Street** - named for John Houstoun, one of the delegates to the Second Continental Congress and the first mayor of Savannah.

**Howard Street** - named for John Purple Howard, a philanthropist who was noted for his liberal gifts to public institutions and the poor.

**Hull Street** - named for Isaac Hull, Commander of the U.S.S. Constitution, "Old Ironsides," and a hero of the War of 1812. Formerly Chatham Street. The name was changed in 1815.

**Huntingdon Street** - named for Selina Hastings, Countess of Huntingdon and benefactress to Bethesda Orphanage.

**Indian Street** - named for the road to the village of the Yamacraw Indians.

**Jefferson Street** - named for Thomas Jefferson, third president of the United States.

**Jones Street** - named for Major John Jones of Liberty County who was killed in the Battle of Savannah in 1779.

**Liberty Street** - named in 1801 for the spirit of liberty.

**Lincoln Street** - named for General Benjamin Lincoln, commander of Continental forces in Savannah during the Battle of Savannah in 1779.

**Macon Street** - named for Nathaniel Macon, North Carolina senator and speaker of the house who died in 1837.

**Martin Luther King, Jr. Boulevard** - named for Dr. Martin Luther King, Jr., slain civil rights minister and leader. Prior to the change, the name was West Broad Street. When South Broad was changed to Oglethorpe Avenue in 1897, there was a motion to change West Broad to Tomochichi Avenue, but it failed. Originally the street was West Boundary, signifying the western boundary of the township.

**McDonough Street** - named for Master-Commandant Thomas McDonough, hero of the Battle of Lake Champlain in the War of 1812. Formerly Screven Street. The name was changed in 1815.

**Mercer Street** - named for Hugh W. Mercer, Confederate General from Savannah.

**Montgomery Street** - named for American General Richard Montgomery who fell at the siege of Quebec in 1775.

**Oglethorpe Avenue** - In the early days of the colony it was referred to as "Market Street." It was named South Broad Street in 1801 and in 1897 named for James Edward Oglethorpe, the founder of the colony. The center plats were used as common areas for the settlers and the plat west of Bull Street as a early burial site for Jewish colonists.

**Perry Street** - named for Admiral Oliver Hazard Perry, hero of the Battle of Lake Erie in the War of 1812. Formerly Wilkes Street. The name was changed in 1815.

**President Street** - formerly King Street. Name changed in 1803 after the Revolutionary War to show a freedom from royalty.

**Price Street** - named for Charles Price, member of the General Assembly who served under General Lachlan McIntosh and was killed in the assault on the British in the Battle of Savannah in 1779.

**Randolph Street** - named for John Randolph, the Virginia statesman who was an ardent defender of states' rights.

**Reynolds Street** - named for John Reynolds, the first royal governor of Georgia.

**St. Gall Street** - named for the Swiss town where Presbyterian minister John Zubly was born.

**St. Julian Street** - named for James St. Julian who aided with constructing houses and planting in the early colony.

**State Street** - formerly Prince Street. Name changed in 1803 after the Revolutionary War to show a freedom from royalty.

**Tattnall Street** - named for Josiah Tattnall, Jr., hero of the Revolution and later governor of Georgia.

**Taylor Street** - named for General Zachary Taylor, hero of the Mexican War.

**Waldburg Street** - named for Jacob Waldburg, a prominent citizen.

**Wayne Street** - named for Mayor Richard Wayne.

**Wheaton Street** - named for John F. Wheaton, Captain of the Chatham Artillery and mayor of Savannah. It was formerly the Sea Island road.

**Whitaker Street** - named for Benjamin Whitaker, a South Carolinian who gave 100 cattle to the early colony.

**Williamson Street** - named for John P. Williamson, mayor from 1808-09. It was once known as "Battle Row."

**Wilson Street** - named for Edward G. Wilson, one time clerk of city council.

**York Street** - named for the Duke of York. The town, in a liberal mood, left it unchanged after the Revolution.

**Zubly Street** - named for Reverend John Zubly, Presbyterian minister in Savannah in 1776.

# Cemeteries

## Bonaventure Cemetery
### Bonaventure Road

***Looking toward the river at Bonaventure Cemetery***

The name Bonaventure comes from the Italian "Buona Ventura," for good fortune. It was one of the earliest plantations in Savannah. The land was granted to John Mulryne, an English colonel, in 1760. It was at Bonaventure that Royal Governor James Wright hid from patriot forces during the Revolution. He and Colonel Mulryne fled Georgia, returning to England aboard the Man of War, *Scarborough*.

Within a short time, Mulryne died and the plantation passed to his daughter Mary and her husband, Josiah Tattnall. Tattnall refused to get involved in the war, either with the Americans or the British. Because of this, he was banished to England and the plantation confiscated. His son, Josiah, Jr., returned to fight for the patriots under Nathanael Greene.

Young Josiah so distinguished himself that he was allowed to buy back some of his father's holdings, including Bonaventure. He lived there for 18 active years, serving as a member of the state legislature, a member of Congress, and as governor of Georgia. Josiah, Jr. died in 1804 in the West Indies, having gone there to recapture his health. He was only 38 years old. Josiah had expressed a desire to be buried beside his wife at Bonaventure, and in accordance with his wishes, he was sent home to join her. Tattnall Street and Tattnall County were named in his honor.

In 1847, Peter Wiltberger, owner the Pulaski Hotel, purchased Bonaventure and opened it as a cemetery. It was the Evergreen Cemetery of Bonaventure until title passed to the city in 1907. Since that time it has been known as simply, Bonaventure Cemetery.

In 1867, a young naturalist named John Muir left Louisville, Kentucky walking 1,000 miles to the Florida Keys. When he reached Savannah, he spent five days and nights in Bonaventure. He was so taken with the area he wrote, "The grand old forest graveyard, so impressive that almost any sensible person would choose to dwell here with the dead rather than with the lazy, disorderly living. Never, since I was allowed to walk the woods, have I found such impressive trees as the moss draped oaks of Bonaventure." Muir went on to found the Sierra Club and became the moving force for the creation of Yellowstone and Yosemite as national parks.

**Notable graves:** Little Gracie; philanthropist William Gaston; prominent colonist Noble Jones; patriot Noble Wimberly Jones, Governor Josiah Tattnall, Jr., musical composer Johnny Mercer; Governor Edward Telfair and his daughters Mary and Margaret, writer Conrad Aiken; and the following Confederate officers: Commodore Josiah Tattnall III and Generals Robert H. Anderson, Henry R. Jackson, Alexander R. Lawton, Hugh W. Mercer, and Claudius C. Wilson.

The cemetery is open from dawn to dusk.

## Colonial Park Cemetery
### Abercorn Street and Oglethorpe Avenue

Originally, the burial ground for Christ Church Parish. In 1789 it was enlarged to become the city cemetery for Christian people of all denominations. The Park was closed to further burials in 1853. Colonial Cemetery showcases the many architectural styles used for family vaults during this period..

While Union General Sherman resided in the plush surroundings of the Green-Meldrim House during his occupation of Savannah, many of his troops camped in the cemetery and also used it as a stabling ground. These soldiers ransacked the vaults in search of silver which, according to rumor, had been

*Gate to Colonial Park Cemetery*

hidden in the cemetery. Graves were desecrated with bones and skulls strewn about and quite a few of the headstones scattered. Dozens of grave sites were lost, never to be relocated. Many of the broken tombstones are now cemented against the cemetery's eastern wall.

**Notable graves:** one of the three signers of the Declaration of Independence from Georgia, Button Gwinnett; many early leaders including: Archibald Bulloch, Samuel Elbert, Lachlan McIntosh, William Scarbrough, and James Habersham along with his three sons: James, Jr., Joseph, and John.

Visitors are welcome to explore the cemetery and read the tombstones.

## Jewish Cemetery
### Cohen and Spruce Streets

This burial ground was laid out by Levi de Lyon for the de Lyon - de la Motta families. The space is small containing about 12 graves and only four of those identified. The reason for its small size relates to an incident that occurred soon after it opened.

A Jewish citizen died who was not a member of either of these families. They refused to permit his burial in the cemetery. Upon learning this, Mordecai Sheftall, a prominent citizen, was so angered he purchased a nearby tract of land as a burial place for all Jews.

*Old Jewish Cemetery*

The cemetery is surrounded by a low wall and locked.

## Laurel Grove Cemetery
### Ogeechee Road and Anderson Street

Laurel Grove was part of Springfield Plantation owned by Joseph Stiles. The city acquired the land in 1850 for a cemetery which was opened in 1852. The former use of the property had been as rice fields. Since rice fields were periodically flooded, it was necessary to drain the land before it could be used as grave sites. When Colonial Park Cemetery was closed to further burial, Laurel Grove's 60 acres became the city's primary burial ground.

*The Confederate burial field*

When the cemetery opened, it became quite fashionable for citizens to ride out on Sundays to visit not only the departed, but each other. With this in mind, Laurel Grove was laid out with green spaces and wide lanes for carriages. The iron work around many of the lots is extraordinary and the mausoleums are constructed using many different styles.

One section is designated as a sailor's burial ground "hallowed to the men who go down to the sea in ships and occupy their business in great waters." The plot was for seafarers who died while in the port of Savannah. Present are ships' captains and seamen from all over the world. Each year, a commemorative service is held for the officers and men of the merchant marine who lie here. The service is the Sunday nearest National Maritime Day, May 22nd, of each year.

**Notable graves:** the Confederate soldier's burial field with 622 dead, many of whom fell at Gettysburg. The statute *"Silence,"* that originally stood as the lower part of the Confederate Monument in Forsyth Park, overlooks the fallen soldiers. Confederate generals Francis S. Bartow, Jeremy F. Gilmer, Paul

J. Harrison, Sr., Peter McGlashan, Lafayette McLaws, Gilbert Moxley Sorrel, and Henry C. Wayne are here. Many notable Savannahians are also here: Juliette Gordon Low, founder of the Girl Scouts; Florence Martus, the waving girl; James Pierpont, composer of "Jingle Bells," and John MacPherson Berrien, U.S. Senator and attorney general under President Andrew Jackson. Berrien County was named in his honor. James Moore Wayne, associate justice of the U.S. Supreme Court is here. Other notable graves are: Charles Hart Olmstead, commanding officer at Fort Pulaski during its bombardment by Union troops; The Right Reverend Stephen Elliot, Georgia's first Episcopal Bishop and a founder of the University of the South at Sewanee, Tennessee; and Phoebe Pember, commemorated on a U.S. postage stamp. She was in charge of the Chimborazo Hospital in Richmond during the last days of the Civil War. They had dispensed care to 76,000 southern soldiers. Phoebe was the last Confederate official remaining in Richmond, protecting her patients with a pistol when the Union army arrived. There is also a monument to the dead of the Spanish-American War.

Visitors are welcome.

## Laurel Grove Cemetery - South
### 37th Street - West of Ogeechee Road

The connector road from 37th Street to Interstate 16 divided Laurel Grove into two cemeteries. The southern portion is dedicated to Savannah's black community.

*Rev. Andrew Bryan and Andrew Cox Marshall*

**Notable graves:** the final resting place for many prominent black Savannahians including the Reverend Andrew Bryan, early pastor of the First African Baptist Church. There is also a large memorial stone to the Reverend Andrew Cox Marshall, pastor of the First African Baptist Church during its construction, who died at 100 years of age. Buried here are members of the DeVeaux family which produced the country's first black customs official.

Visitors are welcome

## Sheftall Cemetery

### Cohen and Garrard Streets (One block south of the Jewish Cemetery)

*Sheftall Cemetery*

This cemetery was opened on a tract acquired in 1773 by Mordecai Sheftall and used until about 1860.

The reported story is that Sheftall secured the land because he was angry that the two families who controlled the Jewish Cemetery nearby were not permitting burial for persons outside their immediate clan. Burial was permitted here for all persons professing the Jewish religion.

Currently, it is under the care of Temple Mickve Israel and means for its upkeep have been provided by the Sheftall family.

**Notable graves:** The oldest tomb is that of Mordecai Sheftall who arrived in the colony in 1733 and died in 1797. Apparently the cemetery was not active for a period after its initial opening in 1773. Sheftall "Cocked Hat" Sheftall is also buried here.

The cemetery is enclosed by a high concrete wall and a locked gate. Admission is not possible.

# Forts

## Fort Frederica
### St. Simons Island, Georgia

*Fort Frederica at St. Simon's*

This outpost served as Oglethorpe's southern defense against the Spanish in Florida. It was laid out in 1736 and named for Frederick, Prince of Wales and eldest son of King George II.

Shortly after the fort was erected, England and Spain collided in what has been called "The War of Jenkins Ear." The name comes from Thomas Jenkins, a British smuggler, whose ear was severed by Spanish soldiers when they captured the English brig, *Rebecca.* The Spanish told him to take his ear and show it to the king. Jenkins appeared before Parliament holding his severed ear aloft to prove how Englishmen were mistreated. This incident played right into England's hands. With avarice, they had been eying the Spanish holdings in Florida and this was just the excuse they needed to attack.

Oglethorpe returned to England for the second time. This trip was to raise troops for the coming war against the Spanish. King George appointed him commander-in-chief of all British forces in Georgia and South Carolina. Oglethorpe asked Charleston for soldiers but South Carolina was very reluctant, having become jealous of Georgia. They finally responded with 500 troops who were intent on the prospect of plunder. Oglethorpe's efforts in England were successful and he returned with more than 600 men. However, some were Catholics and held Spanish sympathies. In a surprise revolt, they attempted to assassinate Oglethorpe and turn the colony over to

Spain. The uprising failed and the ringleader was speedily shot.

Oglethorpe sailed into St. Augustine with his strong force and quickly sacked the town but was unable to overcome the fort. He withdrew and returned to Frederica. The Spanish quickly retaliated, landing on St. Simons Island with more than 3,000 men from 36 ships. Two detachments were sent overland to find the best approach to Fort Frederica. Whilc one group marched single file through a dense forest, Oglethorpe's troops attacked. Many Spanish were killed and the remainder retreated to the ships.

When they returned with reinforcements, Oglethorpe's forces had vanished. Actually, they pulled back to set an ambush in the open marsh on St. Simons. When the Spanish troops reached the marsh, believing they were on safe ground, they began preparing for dinner. With surprise on their side, Oglethorpe's small unit swooped out of the marsh and drove the invaders into full rout. The Spanish loss in dead, wounded, and prisoners was estimated at more than 500. The spot is now known as the "Battle of Bloody Marsh."

Oglethorpe was still not through. Next, he tricked the Spanish into thinking he was expecting heavy reinforcements. They retreated and sailed back to Florida to never again attack the English colonies. Oglethorpe received letters of congratulations from almost all the governors in the colonies with the exception of South Carolina. With the Spanish threat gone, the garrison at Frederica was transferred and most of the town abandoned.

Oglethorpe preferred Frederica to Savannah and made it home for his remaining time in Georgia. His estate was known as the "cottage" and occupied 500 acres of land. It was all returned to the Crown when he left the colony for the final time in 1743.

## Fort Jackson

### President Street Extension two miles east of Savannah

The oldest standing fort in Georgia, originally the location of a Revolutionary War earthen battery. All boats entering Savannah had to pass this point. The marshes surrounding the fort offered defense from a ground attack and deep anchorage near the shore allowed easy shipment of supplies and troop movement. Troops were garrisoned here during the War of 1812 and the facility was rebuilt in 1842.

Fort Jackson was occupied by Confederate troops during the Civil

War until Savannah was captured by General Sherman. Union troops immediately occupied the fort but they received a parting shot from the *C.S.S. Savannah* before it was exploded to avoid capture. It was the only time the

***Fort Jackson***

fort received hostile fire.

Fort Jackson was named in honor of Colonel James Jackson. Jackson was an active member of the Liberty Boys who joined their raid on the powder magazine in 1775 and participated in burning rice boats to avoid their falling into British hands. During the siege of Savannah, he was a favorite of Admiral D'Estaing and came to the attention of General Nathanael Greene. Just in his twenties, he rose to the rank of colonel and was selected by General "Mad Anthony" Wayne to receive the British surrender of Savannah in 1783.

Famous for his many duels, his pistols were rarely cool. Many felt his death was due to an accumulation of wounds received during a lifetime on the field of honor. Thomas Spalding said, "he was the noblest man with whom it has been my lot to be acquainted."

Jackson refused his first chance at a governorship on the grounds of his youth, but accepted his election as a U.S. Senator. In the 1790's he did serve as governor. Jackson died in Washington, D.C. in 1806 and is buried there in the Congressional Cemetery. Jackson County was also named in his honor.

Today, the fort offers both a Maritime Museum and a Black Military

History Museum. Among its demonstrations is the firing of the largest black powder cannon in the United States. The fort is open to the public.

## Fort McAllister
### Richmond Hill

Built in 1861 and named after Colonel George Washington McAllister. McAllister owned Strathy-Hall Plantation in Bryan County as well as the property on which the fort was built.

The fort's purpose was guarding the rear entry to Savannah during the

***Storming Fort McAllister***

Civil War. It was at a prime location to deny access to the Ogeechee River by Union boats, protect a vital railroad trestle, and defend the river's rice plantations from Union raids. Among the fort's arsenal was a "hotshot gun" that fired red-hot cannonballs hoping to set wooden ships on fire. Unfortunately, the fort's guns were unable to reach the Union ships that stayed out of range firing their new rifled long-range cannon.

The earthen work fort successfully defended seven assaults from the sea. Probably the most memorable was against the ironclad *Montauk* that was armed with a 15-inch cannon, the largest mounted on a ship to that date. It was commanded by John L. Worden, who captained the *Monitor* when it clashed with the Confederate *Merrimac*. The ensuing five-hour barrage on Fort McAllister ended in a standoff. The following month, Worden led another attack in which the fort's commander, Major John B. Gallie of Savannah, was killed. His was the fort's only fatality during all the bombardments it suffered. He is buried in Laurel Grove Cemetery.

Fort McAllister was finally captured when attacked from land by General Sherman's army on his "March to the Sea." As the fort commander, Major George W. Anderson, was fond of saying, "The fort never surrendered, it was captured by overwhelming numbers." Overwhelming indeed, 3,500 men from Sherman's army to 150 Confederates. The fighting became hand-to-hand in a fierce battle lasting only 15 minutes. Major Anderson is also buried in Laurel Grove Cemetery.

The fort is open to visitors. There is a park that has a 1.3 mile walking trail, dock and boat ramps, tent and trailer sites, and picnic and fishing areas.

## Fort Pulaski

### Cockspur Island - 14 miles east of Savannah on U.S. Highway 80

Cockspur Island takes its name from the shape of a dangerous reef that juts out toward the open sound. The island is in sight of the Atlantic Ocean and the fort guards the two entrances to the Savannah River. Fort Pulaski was the third fort to be built here. First was Fort George and second was Fort Greene, both during revolutionary times. Fort Pulaski was named for Count Casimir Pulaski who was killed at the Battle of Savannah during the Revolutionary War.

The fort was built between 1829 and 1847. Erection of the facility was the first assignment for young Robert E. Lee, freshly graduated from West Point. The fort has five sides with brick walls 11 feet thick, enclosing a 2½ acre parade ground. All of this is surrounded by a wide moat that must be crossed by a drawbridge. Fort Pulaski was designed to withstand any attack and was constructed using 25 million bricks. Many of these came from the Hermitage Plantation upriver from the fort. Early in the construction process,

*Fort Pulaski*

they discovered the soft mud of the island would not support the weight of the fort. The weight of the walls had to be reduced and heavy wooden pilings driven 70 feet into the mud to support the load.

At the outbreak of the Civil War, Lee returned to examine the fort in his capacity as inspector of the southern coastal defenses. The fort was the ultimate in defense systems and considered impregnable. That logic soon vanished as it fell to Union forces in April 1862 when they used rifled cannons for the first time in warfare. The batteries were fired from locations on Tybee Island more than a mile away. It's been said that generals always prepare for the preceding war and Fort Pulaski was a good example. After 5,275 shells and a little more than 30 hours, the thick walls were breached. Shells flying through the gap threatened to ignite the fort's magazine which was directly opposite the breach and contained 40,000 pounds of powder.

Faced with annihilation, Colonel Charles H. Olmstead, 25 years of age, surrendered to avoid needless loss of the 385 defenders under his command. At the surrender ceremony, he said to the Union officer, Major James G. Halpine, "I yield my sword. I trust I have not disgraced it." The sword was kept in the north by the Halpine family as a souvenir for 117 years. Finally, it was returned to the fort and is on display. The captured Confederate defenders were sent to Governor's Island, New York for imprisonment, with many of the sick and wounded dying there.

Some damage to the walls was left unrepaired to illustrate the fury of the attack. Fort Pulaski was proclaimed a national monument in 1924 and is now operated by the U.S. Park Service. It is open for tours.

## Fort Screven
### Tybee Island

*Fort Screven at Tybee Island*

Completed in 1896 as Fort Tybee. The name was changed to Fort Graham for Brigadier General William Montrose Graham, commander of Atlantic coast defenses. It was changed again in 1899 to honor Brigadier General James Screven of the Georgia Militia, a Revolutionary War hero who was killed in action near Midway, Georgia in 1776. He was shot from his horse and several British soldiers fired their rifles into him. Screven was taken to Midway Church for medical treatment and later transferred to a private home where he died. He was only 28 years old. He is buried in the Midway Congregational Church Cemetery. Screven County was also named in his honor.

The fort was manned during the Spanish-American War, World War

I, and World War II. One of its more notable commanders was General George C. Marshall and at one time it was home to a young Captain Dwight D. Eisenhower. Originally, it was a coast artillery fort, later an infantry post, and finally a military school for deep sea diving, the only one offered by the army in America.

For 50 years Fort Screven was a powerful coastal defense base with the most massive concrete emplacements on the Atlantic seaboard, housing 20 inch guns and mortars. The construction required 300,000 cubic yards of cement that was barged downriver to the fort.

The Eighth Infantry was stationed here after its return from Germany in 1923. In 1940 the Coastal Artillery Corps took control and at the end of WWII, the War Department declared the fort surplus and it was sold to the town of Tybee. Many of the original houses known as "Officer's Row," still keep their vigil on the old parade ground.

## Fort Wayne
### East Broad and Bay Streets

*Fort Wayne on Bay and East Broad Streets*

In early days, it was a favorite meeting place for duelists. Originally it was known as Fort Savannah and constructed during the Revolutionary War. The fort was manned for defense against the British attack led by Colonel Archibald Campbell in 1778. Because of its vantage point, it was well situated to defend against enemy boats coming up the river. The fort was renamed for General "Mad Anthony" Wayne following the Revolutionary War. Wayne was given the "Mad Anthony" moniker after friends witnessed his reckless courage in battle.

*"Mad Anthony" Wayne*

Wayne was born in 1745 at Waynesboro, Pennsylvania. His proficiency in school was greater in feats of mock warfare than his classroom studies. When the Revolutionary War broke out, he was appointed colonel of Continental forces in Pennsylvania. Youth and lack of formal training in the military alienated him from many of his fellow officers. Although he was impetuous, he could fight as well as brag. Wayne spent the winter in Valley Forge with George Washington who readily admitted to his bravery and self possession in battle, but feared his rashness of action.

After the British surrender at Yorktown, Wayne was sent by General Nathanael Greene to Georgia to oust the remainder of British hostiles. In 1783, at war's end, he retired from active service as a major general. Georgia acknowledged its appreciation to Wayne by granting him an 800-acre rice plantation. He borrowed the necessary funds for its operation from Dutch creditors who subsequently were forced to foreclose on the land.

Wayne was elected to congress as a representative from Georgia but only served from 1791-1792. His seat was declared vacant due to irregularities in residence qualifications since he was still active in business in

Pennsylvania at the time. He died in Erie, Pennsylvania in 1796. Wayne County was named in his honor.

The Fort Wayne site was acquired by the Savannah Gas Company in 1850. The retaining wall was added when Bay Street was extended by the city.

# Historic Churches

Much of the information in this section was taken from *"Higher Ground: Historic Churches and Synagogues in Savannah,"* by Rita F. Spitler.

## The Cathedral of St. John the Baptist
### Lafayette Square

***Cathedral of St. John the Baptist***

When the colony was in its infancy, the trustees feared the Catholics would have a greater loyalty to the Spanish in Florida than to England. For this reason, Catholics weren't allowed to settle in Savannah until after the Revolutionary War.

This church was organized in 1796. The first building was erected on Liberty Square and the congregation worshiped there until the present edifice was completed. The Victorian Gothic Cathedral by Francis Baldwin was begun in 1873 and finally completed in 1896. The same year, it burned and was almost destroyed. The cathedral was rebuilt using the same design and reopened in 1899. It is the second oldest Roman Catholic Church in Georgia and the seat of the Diocese of Savannah.

## Christ Episcopal Church
### Johnson Square

Christ Church is often referred to as the "Mother Church of Georgia." It was on February 12, 1733, the day the colony was founded, that the first service was held. The church stands on its original site. The current structure, completed in 1840, is the fourth building on this location. It was fashioned in the manner of a Roman temple by its architect, James Hamilton Couper and designed in the Greek Revival style. A bell, forged in 1819 in Boston, by Revere and Son, hangs in the northeast tower. Inside the chancel area is a large stained glass window depicting the ascension of Christ.

*Christ Episcopal Church*

It was here in 1736, that John Wesley started the first Sunday school and published the first English hymnal used in America. In 1738, George Whitefield succeeded John Wesley as minister. He was one of the most eloquent evangelists of his time and a spark for the "Great Awakening" revival of the mid 1700's. Whitefield was a founder of Bethesda Orphanage in Savannah.

*Beth Eden Baptist Church*

## Beth Eden Baptist Church

### Lincoln and Gordon Streets

Beth Eden resulted from a split with the Second African Baptist Church in 1890. In 1897, the present structure was built. It is a Victorian Gothic design by Henry Urban, an English architect.

# First African Baptist Church
## Franklin Square

The origin of this church can be traced back to George Leile and his preaching to fellow slaves along the Savannah River in 1775. He gained his freedom from slavery in 1777 and was evacuated by the British in 1782 to Jamaica. While in Savannah, Leile baptized Andrew Bryan, a slave and coachman of Jonathan Bryan, on the grounds of Brampton Plantation.

***First African Baptist Church***

Andrew Bryan was born in South Carolina in 1716 and ordained in 1788. He was imprisoned and whipped for preaching at a time when whites feared any slave gathering as a focus for rebellion. But Bryan persevered and finally was able to purchase both his and his family's freedom. He strived to find a permanent home for his congregation and was able to purchase a lot on Bryan Street (now site of First Bryan Baptist Church) in 1793. Bryan was pastor for 24 years until his death in 1812. He is buried in Laurel Grove Cemetery - South.

The first service for the church was on January 20, 1788, with 67 in attendance. It is the oldest black congregation in America. After property was acquired on Bryan Street, they worshiped there until 1832 when the congregation split into two factions. The First African group moved to Franklin Square while others remained to eventually become First Bryan Baptist Church.

The current edifice on the square was built by slaves in 1859. The work was permitted after they completed their duties for the day. The church has remarkable stained glass windows depicting important figures in its history. The original bell tower, five times taller than the one in use today, was lost to a hurricane in the early 1900's. The flooring contains holes in a decorative pattern that provided air for runaway slaves that were often hidden underneath. Some of the pews have been marked with native African symbols by past members.

## First Baptist Church
### Chippewa Square

The congregation was organized in 1800 and moved to its present location in 1833. It was known for years as the Savannah Baptist Church. The design is classic Greek Revival and is constructed with limestone stucco over Savannah gray brick. It has been called the Parthenon of Savannah. It is the oldest original church building in the city and was designed by Elias Carter. Reverend William B. Johnson, one of the early pastors, wrote much of the constitution in 1845 for the formation of the Southern Baptist Convention and served as its first president. Another of its ministers, Reverend Jesse Mercer, founded Mercer University in Macon from a bequest left by Josiah Penfield, one of the church deacons.

***First Baptist Church***

## First Bryan Baptist Church
### 575 W. Bryan Street

This location dates back to 1793 and is said to be the oldest parcel of black owned real estate in the country. Originally, it was the site of the First African Baptist Church.

The congregation of First African split in 1832, when First African moved to Franklin Square.

***First Bryan Baptist Church***

The other faction of the congregation remained in the original location and became First Bryan. The present structure, built in 1873, was designed by John B. Hogg who had earlier drawn similar plans for Trinity United Methodist Church.

## First Congregational Church
### Whitefield Square

The church dates back to 1869, two years after the Beach Institute was founded. The Institute was established after the Civil War for the education of blacks in Savannah. Several students and 13 missionary teachers from the North began worship services at the school. In 1878 the present site was acquired and a building erected in 1895.

*First Congregational Church*

Although it began as part of the Congregational Church, it is today affiliated with the United Church of Christ. This denomination was formed by a merger of the Congregational Christian Church and the Evangelical and Reformed Church.

## Independent Presbyterian Church
### Bull Street and Oglethorpe Avenue

The congregation was organized in 1755 but it was not until 1816, that John Holden Green of Rhode Island was commissioned to design the present structure. The actual construction was done by Amos Scudder who hauled by wagon the marble flagstones from his farm in New Jersey. The original building burned in the fire of 1889 but today's replica, by William G. Preston, is the same Neoclassical style. It is thought to be one of Savannah's most notable buildings. The massive steeple, made of steel and cast iron, weighs 180 tons. Each of the four interior columns represents a single tree trunk. In accordance with a bequest from Mary Telfair, both the high pulpit and gallery must always remain materially unchanged.

Lowell Mason, school master and composer, came to Savannah in 1820 when he was only twenty years of age to serve as the church organist. He remained for seven years before returning to Massachusetts. His hymns include *"Nearer, My God, to Thee," "When I Survey the Wondrous Cross," and "My Faith Looks Up to Thee."*

***Independent Presbyterian Church***

Ellen Louise Axson, whose grandfather was a minister of the church, was born in the manse of this church in 1860. She was married here in 1885 to Woodrow Wilson who later became the president of the United States.

***Lutheran Church of the Ascension***

## Lutheran Church of the Ascension

### Wright Square

On April 12, 1741, Johann Bolzius, one of the two pastors of the New Jerusalem Lutheran Church at Ebenezer, conducted services for this congregation. In 1771 the present lot was deeded to the church. The congregation purchased the wooden courthouse on the adjacent trust lot and transported it using rollers across President Street to the current site. A steeple and a bell were added and services were begun in the restructured building.

It was customary in the Lutheran church for men and women to sit apart in gender segregated sections. Most of the early services were conducted in German and it was not until 1824 that services were delivered in English. The current Gothic building dates from 1844 but was substantially altered in 1875 when the Ascension Window behind the pulpit was installed. The Rose Window above the front entrance depicts Martin Luther with his coat of arms. Undoubtedly, it is one of Savannah's most dramatic church interiors.

## St. John's Episcopal Church

### Madison Square

The church was begun in 1841 as an expansion parish of Christ Church by Stephen Elliott, Jr., Georgia's first Episcopal bishop. He served as its first rector while still maintaining his ministerial duties at Christ Church.

The current building, in Gothic Revival style, dates from 1853 and was designed by Calvin N. Otis of Buffalo, N.Y. It is known for its 47 bell chimes that have been heard by the community since 1854. The congregation maintains the old order of the Episcopal faith, using the unrevised prayer book and hymnal.

*St. John's Episcopal Church*

## St. Paul's Greek Orthodox Church

### Bull and Anderson Streets

The church was chartered in 1907 with its congregation moving to the present location in 1941. The building was erected in 1898 as "Lawton Hall," a memorial to General Alexander Robert Lawton and his daughter, Corinne, who died prematurely.

Lawton commanded Confederate troops that fought with Stonewall Jackson at Antietam during the Civil War. His brigade suffered 50 percent casualties in that battle and Lawton was so severely wounded, he was reassigned to serve as quartermaster general of the army. At war's end, he accompanied Jefferson Davis in his flight from Richmond and was with him when the government was dissolved at Washington, Georgia. Lawton is buried in Bonaventure Cemetery.

***St. Paul's Greek Orthodox Church***

The building was initially intended for the use, benefit, and advantage of the public. It was used for meetings and concerts until 1941, when it was purchased by the church.

## Second African Baptist Church

### Greene Square

The second oldest black Baptist church in North America, organized December 26, 1802. It was in this church, in January 1865, that Union General Rufus Saxon read Lincoln's Emancipation Proclamation to the newly freed slaves. Here too, was where Dr. Martin Luther King, Jr. gave his famous *"I have a dream"* sermon, later made memorable during his march on Washington, D.C.

***Second African Baptist Church***

## Temple Mickve Israel
### Monterey Square

*Temple Mickve Israel*

This is the third oldest congregation in the United States practicing Reformed Judaism. It was founded by a group of Jews, mainly of Spanish-Portuguese extraction, that arrived in Savannah just five months after Oglethorpe landed with the original colonists. The congregation was formed by the Abraham Minis and Benjamin Sheftall families as K.K. Mickva Israel (Hope of Israel). The families brought with them a "Sephar Torah," (scriptures) still treasured by the congregation. The present structure was developed from a sketch by Henry G. Harrison and consecrated in 1878. It is the only purely Gothic Revival synagogue in America. The Mordecai Sheftall Memorial Hall, adjacent to the temple, houses numerous artifacts and historical data including letters from several U.S. Presidents.

## Trinity United Methodist Church
### Telfair Square

Trinity began as Wesley Chapel in 1812 at Lincoln Street and Oglethorpe Avenue. It is the oldest Methodist congregation in Savannah. The present sanctuary, designed by John B.

*Trinity United Methodist Church*

Hogg, was completed in 1850 in the Greek Revival style. A fire in 1991 caused major damage to the building but it was restored and reopened in 1993. The interior is similar to the Wesley Chapel in London.

## Unitarian Universalist Church
### Troup Square

The Unitarian Society was formed in Savannah in 1831. In 1851 a building was erected by the Unitarians with funds donated by Moses Eastman, the jeweler. Eastman died in 1850 and the church was completed by his widow, Eliza. It was a Gothic structure designed by John S. Norris and built on Oglethorpe Square on the northwest trust lot.

***Unitarian Universalist Church***

In 1852, the Reverend John Pierpont, Jr. arrived from the north and was joined by his brother, James, the following year. James served as church organist and choir director and is remembered mainly for his popular winter composition "*Jingle Bells*," copyrighted in 1859. Their father was a staunch abolitionist and strongly urged John to preach against slavery. Obviously, this was an unpopular stand in the South and created many empty pews among the congregation. The brothers were soon forced out.

The church disbanded in 1860 due to sectional pressures and the building was returned to Mrs. Eastman. She in turn sold the structure to the Episcopal Church of Georgia who moved it to its present location on Troup Square. There, it became St. Stephens, the first parish for African Americans in Georgia. That congregation sold the building in 1943 to the Baptist Church and it became the home of the Savannah Baptist Center.

It was not until the 1950's, during the civil rights era, that the Unitarian congregation was regenerated and strengthened by the merger with the national Universalists. In 1997, the Baptist Center moved to a new location and the Unitarians were able to reclaim their old church building. On

Easter Sunday, 1997, they marched from Columbia Square to Troup Square to reoccupy their facility.

## Wesley Monumental United Methodist Church

### Calhoun Square

This church is a monument to John and Charles Wesley, the founders of Methodism. It was organized in 1868 as a mission of Trinity Methodist.

The sanctuary, patterned after Queen's Kirk in Amsterdam, was completed in 1890. The Wesley window, facing Abercorn Street, contains the busts of John and Charles Wesley. The stained glass windows were assembled in the world famous studio of Louis Tiffany and were installed in 1890 by Tiffany personally. He came from New York and devoted several months to the project.

***Wesley Monumental United Methodist Church***

The Gothic Revival building is said to be one of the handsomest Methodist Churches in the South. Among church artifacts, is a silver communion chalice said to have been used by John Wesley during his tenure in Savannah.

# Places of Interest

## Bethesda Home for Boys
### Whitefield and Ferguson Avenues

*Bethesda Orphanage in Savannah*

The idea of establishing an orphanage in Georgia was suggested by Charles Wesley and James Oglethorpe and enthusiastically embraced by the Reverend George Whitefield. Whitefield arrived in the colony in 1738 with his friend James Habersham to help oversee the project. They called it Bethesda, which means "House of Mercy." Whitefield was a tireless worker, a powerful preacher, and one of the most well known men of his day. Through his efforts, substantial funds were raised and in 1739, a grant of 500 acres was obtained from the trustees of the colony. This began a 32-year quest of raising money for Bethesda that saw Whitefield cross the Atlantic 13 times and preach an estimated 18,000 sermons. That averages out to about ten a week. Whitefield's interest in the institution he founded never flagged. During his lifetime, he paid frequent visits to what he called: "my beloved

Bethesda, surely the most delightful place in all the southern part of America." Habersham served as the administrator and educator and also substituted as a preacher when Whitefield was away.

The site of the orphanage, about 15 miles south of Savannah, was selected by James Habersham with the idea that it would be far away from the "wicked influence of the town." He said "the boys and girls will be taught to labor for their souls as well as for their daily bread."

In March 1740, Whitefield laid the first brick for the orphanage. The buildings were completed that year and the original 61 residents were taken from Savannah to Bethesda on a road said to be the first constructed anywhere in Georgia. Since then, hundreds of young people have gone forth from Bethesda to make their mark in the world. Among them were Governor John Milledge and General Lachlan McIntosh.

The effort to make the orphanage self sufficient was disappointing and both Whitefield and Habersham became active in the movement to allow slaves in Georgia. Slavery, they felt, would enable Bethesda to be self supporting. To prove his point, Whitefield bought a 640-acre plantation in South Carolina which he named Providence. Providence was extremely successful and it was partly due to Whitefield's example that slavery was approved in Georgia.

In the course of his travels back to England, Whitefield became the personal Chaplain to Selina Hastings, Countess of Huntingdon. She was a distant cousin of George Washington and wrote him concerning the Georgia orphanage. She never came to the colonies but collected great

***The Countess of Huntingdon***

sums of money in England for the orphanage, both during Whitefield's lifetime and after his death in 1770. His will left Bethesda in trust to the Countess Huntingdon and the Georgia legislature passed a bill allowing her to hold property in the province.

Selina became very involved in supporting the school when James Habersham succeeded Whitefield in the management of Bethesda. In 1773 fire and lightning damaged the main building and repairs were made as a result of her benevolence. After one of the fires at the home, she even sold her jewelry to help rebuild the orphanage. The Countess also sent a life-size, full-length portrait of herself to the school.

Her plans to establish a college at Bethesda were thwarted by the American Revolution. During that period, since the Countess was British, the Georgia House of Assembly appointed trustees to manage the property. Amusingly, British troops in the area spared the orphanage because of Selina's portrait, thinking the school still had allegiance to England.

In 1788, again under the patronage of the Countess of Huntingdon, Bethesda did open as a college. Selina died in 1791 at the age of 84. Following her death, the state again assumed control of the property. Huntingdon Street was named in her honor.

During the next ten years, Bethesda fell into decay. Revived in 1801, the school changed its policy and became an orphanage for boys only. It was closed four years later following a disastrous fire.

In 1855 the Union Society acquired the property and recommenced the great work begun by the Reverend Whitefield. The present building was built in 1855 by the Union Society, trustees of Bethesda, and has been in continuous use since 1867. The Union Society was founded in 1750 as the St. George's Club, named after England's patron saint. At some time prior to 1768, its name was changed to the Union Society. It was renamed in honor of three of its known founders. The organization was a charitable pursuit of a Catholic, a Protestant, and a Jew: Peter Tondee, Richard Milledge, and Benjamin Sheftall. From the beginning, the organization took a deep interest in Bethesda. The Society got involved because several of its members had been raised at the orphanage. After Bethesda was closed in 1805, the Society carried a considerable share of the burden of educating orphan children in the community, while still maintaining its other charitable work. Past presidents of the Society include Mordecai Sheftall, George Houstoun, Noble Jones, Joseph Clay, Joseph Habersham, David Mitchell,

John McPherson Berrien, and Richard Arnold. The Union Society still provides the primary support for Bethesda.

The orphanage became a Confederate hospital during the Civil War and was again spared due to a fortuitous misunderstanding. When foraging Union troops were burning area plantations, they encountered a black caretaker at the gates of Bethesda. They asked, "who owns this property? The Union Society," said the caretaker. "Imagine finding loyal sentiment in the heart of the rebellion," said the surprised officer and ordered his men to march on. Bethesda operates today as a home for boys.

## City Market Area

### St. Julian Street between Franklin and Ellis Squares

***Looking West from Ellis Square at City Market***

The buildings are former warehouses and feed and seed stores that were located close to the Old City Market in Ellis Square. A series of market buildings occupied the square with the last being built in 1870. That market was demolished in 1953 to make room for a parking garage. Most of the area buildings are now in use as studios, galleries, shops, clubs, and restaurants. The market is also the place to begin a leisurely tour by horse-drawn carriage through the streets of Savannah. Many times there are bands playing in the piazza for visitor's enjoyment.

## Factor's Walk

### Between Bay and River Streets

Factors were agents for the plantation owners who sold rice, cotton, and other goods. They were also brokers for the naval stores (turpentine,

*Looking East on Factor's Walk*

pitch, and rosin) that passed through the port. Their buildings were built on River Street with the upper floors rising above the Bay Street level. The factors preferred their offices on the higher level and pedestrian bridges were needed for access from Bay Street. The lower floors, fronting on River Street, had multilevel entrances along the ramps to the bluff and were used as warehouses. Many of these buildings still have the central shaft used for the raising and lowering of cotton from the upper levels to the large bay doors on River Street. From there the cotton was loaded on merchant ships to supply the teeming textile industry in England.

A lane called Factor's Walk ran between the buildings and the bluff. The arched pedestrian walkways were built between the second and third stories of the buildings and the sidewalks on Bay Street. The buildings were designed by many different architects and today serve a variety of uses ranging from offices to historic inns.

## The Hermitage Plantation

### About one mile west of the city on the Savannah River

*The Hermitage Plantation*

Henry McAlpin migrated from Scotland to Savannah by way of Charleston in 1804. In 1815 he acquired 230 acres of land on the Savannah River about one mile west of what is now the historic district of Savannah. His training included the study of architecture and engineering but his greatest assets were his intelligence and management skills.

On the plantation was a cast iron foundry, the source of much of the city's decorative ironwork. Shortly after fire had swept the city in 1820, McAlpin and young William Jay formed an association to promote the construction of Savannah houses using iron rather than timber for joists and other primary support. McAlpin's association with Jay probably explains the many Jay characteristics of the mansion built on the property. It was said to be one of the handsomest plantations in Georgia.

McAlpin turned the Hermitage into a model of efficiency. Oddly, it was the only plantation on the river to gain prominence through industrial development rather than agriculture. McAlpin erected one of the first steam-powered saw mills with an engine thought to have been built by James Watt. The Hermitage was also the primary producer of bricks used in many of the historic houses in Savannah in addition to Fort Pulaski. The bricks were used to construct the Central of Georgia Railway station as well as the

Champion-McAlpin house. The spur line laid by McAlpin to carry his bricks to the river for transport is said to be the oldest railroad in the country. The plantation required more than 400 slaves housed in more than 70 brick cabins. At his death in 1851, McAlpin had expanded the Hermitage more than six times its original size and owned several other plantations scattered throughout the South.

The Civil War took a heavy toll on the Hermitage and it never recovered. Ten years after McAlpin's death, the plantation was heavily in debt and mortgaged to banker Aaron Champion. After the war, the famous plantation was sold at auction with Champion being the highest bidder. He placed it with James McAlpin, his son-in-law, in trust for his daughter, Maria and the five McAlpin children. The family ownership continued until 1935 when the house was purchased by Henry Ford. He dismantled the place brick by brick and reconstructed the house with the same plan and brick in Richmond Hill, 15 miles south of Savannah. It was then used as Ford's summer home. The house still remains on the Ogeechee River as a private residence. The Hermitage land was then leased to Union Camp for a paper mill that has remained on the site. McAlpin is buried in Laurel Grove Cemetery.

## Mulberry Grove Plantation

### West of Port Wentworth on the Savannah River

Mulberry Grove consisted of 2,170 acres of rich river land. Prior to the Revolutionary War, it was the home of Lt. Governor John Graham, an English Loyalist. After the war, the land was confiscated and given to General Nathanael Greene, second in command of the American forces, by a grateful government. Greene died of sunstroke within a year of taking possession of the estate. Mulberry later gained notoriety as the site where Eli Whitney invented the cotton gin in

*Caty Littlefield Greene*

1793 while a guest on the plantation.

As Sherman's army approached Savannah during the Civil War, the house was set afire and reduced to ruins by advance scouts. Today the land is owned by the Georgia Ports Authority and is not accessible to the public.

***River Street Houses***

## River Street

### Martin Luther King, Jr. Boulevard to General McIntosh Boulevard

Daily, a train known as the *"River Street Rambler,"* runs down the center of the street on its way to the industrial area on the eastern side of town. The tracks run amid a street paved with ballast stone. Early sailing ships use these stones to give them added weight when they were not fully laden. The stones rendered the stability necessary in heavy seas. As cargo was taken on in Savannah, some of the ballast could be removed. Excess stone was used for paving of River Street and the ramps. These became some of the first paved streets in the city. This stone is used all along the bluff between Bay Street and River Street on the steep stairs and ramps that lead down to the river. About 1850, the stones were also used to shore up the walls of the bluff.

The waterfront is ten city-blocks of walkways and parks lined with some of the most charming and original boutiques of arts and crafts in the country. Mixed in among the shops are restaurants and taverns, some with a good view of the river and others walled with ballast stone or old brick. From these clubs emanate the lyrical notes of blues, jazz, and bluegrass drifting out to the street to entice the strollers as they pass by. The iron balconies extending from many of the buildings assisted the factors in staying attuned to the pulse of the river.

River Street is also host to many festivals including First Saturday, held the first weekend of each month. Arts and crafts from all over the southeast are featured. The eastern end of the street played host to the opening and closing ceremonies for the sailing events of the 1996 Olympics.

***Looking East on River Street***

## Savannah and Ogeechee Canal Park
### Georgia Highway 204 - two miles west of I-95

The canal begins just west of River Street and runs 16.5 miles to the Ogeechee River about two miles west of Interstate 95. It opened in 1831 to bring goods from the Ogeechee Basin and western Chatham County to the port of Savannah for shipment. Like other canals, it used horses to pull flat bottomed barges along its length. In 1848 the canal was renovated and six locks were added. These were four lift locks and two tidal locks.

During the Civil War, invading Union troops caused extensive damage and the canal was temporarily closed. After repairs, it remained active until 1890 when the railroads made the canal obsolete. The entire original route remains intact. Part of the canal can be seen at the Savannah-Ogeechee Canal Park on Route 204, two miles west of I-95.

*Savannah & Ogeechee Canal at the Louisville Road*

## Trustees' Garden

### Southeast corner of East Broad and Bay Streets

The 10-acre tract of land for the garden was cleared within one month of the colonists' settling on the bluff. It was modeled after Chelsea Botanical Garden in London. The trustees were counting on the colony for the cultivation of commodities that England was importing at great expense, especially silk, olive oil, and wine. After all, Georgia was on the same latitude as China, Persia, and the Madeira Islands. Actually, it was the southernmost British colony with the warmest climate and the longest growing season.

The idea was to experiment with plants and herbs from all over the world to determine which ones might have an economic future in Georgia, given the climate and soil condition of the colony. Botanists were sent by the trustees to the West Indies and South America on plant procuring forays. They brought back cuttings of flax, hemp, indigo, and cochineal olives. Medicinal herbs were also grown. Primary emphasis was on making silk production a success. In fact, of each 50 acres of land awarded to the colonists, ten were required to be planted with 100 White Mulberry trees.

One of the first large buildings in the colony was the Filature House on Reynolds Square, constructed for the purpose of reeling silk. Unfortunately, silk production was not feasible in the colony. One problem was that it was too labor intensive to be viable in a frontier society.

***The Filature House***

The first eight pounds of silk ever produced in the colony were sent to Queen Charlotte who wove it into a dress she wore on her birthday. In 1764 more than 15,000 pounds of silk was processed at the filature, over half of which had been processed by the Salzburgers at Ebenezer.

Other crops had more potential. Experiments from this first economic garden in America deemed it feasible to produce the famed upland short staple cotton which later comprised the greater part of the world's cotton commerce. Here also, were propagated the peach trees which became so profitable in both Georgia and South Carolina.

The big problem with some of the plants of which the trustees had high hopes, was the climate of Savannah was not hospitable to tropical cultivation. For example, the grapevines for the wine industry withered in summer while the delicate citrus trees froze in winter. As a result, the garden and the experiments were abandoned after suffering a few of Savannah's infrequent frosts. After this, the highest and best use for the land seemed to be residential expansion. The garden became Georgia's first subdivision, being sold to Governor John Reynolds and subdivided in 1755.

# Tybee Lighthouse
## Northern end of Tybee Island

Oglethorpe realized the survival of the colony was dependent on the safe passage of ships carrying settlers and supplies through the treacherous shoals along the Savannah River. The original lighthouse was a small beacon erected in 1736, which collapsed during a storm in August 1741. It was rebuilt and completed in March 1742. Oglethorpe described it as "much the best building of that kind in America." It was rebuilt in 1757 and again in 1773. Finally in 1783, a masonry lighthouse was constructed on the same spot.

During the Civil War, Union forces occupied Tybee Island as a base of operations against Fort Pulaski. Retreating Confederate forces (the local Irish Jasper Greens) attempted to destroy the building by detonating a keg of

*The Tybee Lighthouse*

gunpowder within the tower. They were only successful in extinguishing the light since the shell of the structure survived. It was rebuilt in 1867 and raised to 154 feet at its highest point. Of the existing lighthouse, the bottom 60 feet is from 1773 and the upper 94 feet from the 1867 rebuilding.

The tower is much the same today as it was after the Civil War. The exterior walls are more than 12 feet thick at the base and taper to about 18 inches at the top. Leading to the observation deck are 178 steps. Tybee Light is the oldest and highest lighthouse in Georgia. It still contains the original Fresnel lens that is nearly eight feet high and magnifies the 30,000 candle-power light so that it can be seen up to 20 miles at sea under ideal conditions.

## Wormsloe

### Richmond Drive and Skidaway Road at Isle of Hope

Constructed by Noble Jones, one of Georgia's first settlers, arriving with James Oglethorpe aboard the ship *Anne* in 1733. Jones was a physician and carpenter in Scurry, England. He served the colony not only as a soldier but as constable, rum agent, and surveyor, laying out the towns of New Ebenezer and Augusta. He also served for 18 years on the Royal Council.

The 500 acres of Wormsloe were originally leased from the trustees but later received by the family in a 1756 royal grant. The property may have been named Wormsloe in honor of the silkworms Jones hoped to cultivate or it could have been named for the Welsh interpretation of "dragon's lair."

A fortification was constructed at Wormsloe between 1739 and 1745 by Noble Jones who commanded a company of marines and was charged with the defense of coastal Georgia. It was designed to protect the inland water approach to Savannah against Spanish attacks from the south. The fort was abandoned when the Jones family built their present house north of the site in 1828. The remains of the fort can still be viewed from the river.

Noble Wimberly Jones, the son of Noble Jones, was called the "Morning Star of Liberty," because of his brilliant and daring services during the Revolution. He was also the first president of the Georgia Medical Society.

The gate marks the entrance to the property and the beginning of a 1.5 mile avenue of live oaks planted in the 1890's to commemorate the birth of Wymberley Wormsloe DeRenne. The gate was erected in 1913 to celebrate his coming of age. A classic marble library stands near the three story mansion in a garden that is unequaled in the South. The property

*The Gate to Wormsloe Plantation*

remained in the family until 1973 when it was acquired by the State of Georgia through the Nature Conservancy. The family retained the house, library, and surrounding gardens. Some areas are open to the public.

## Hutchinson Island
### Across Savannah River from downtown

Named in honor of Archibald Hutchinson, a friend of General Oglethorpe and the early colony. Soon to be the site of a modern trade complex and luxury convention hotel.

# Surrounding Communities

## Ebenezer

### Ga. Highway 275 from Ga. Highway 21 three miles north of Rincon

Ebenezer was founded in 1734 by a group of Austrian Salzburger exiles under the pastoral leadership of Johann Martin Bolzius and Israel Christian Gronau. The town was named Ebenezer by Oglethorpe which means "Stone of Help." It is located about 21 miles up the Savannah River from downtown Savannah. Ebenezer was laid out similar to Savannah, with squares and town lots, but much simpler. One of its functions was to be a northern buffer to Savannah.

The original location was so low and swampy that the settlers asked Oglethorpe for permission to move. He granted their request but with the stipulation that the name of the town not be changed so that he could keep the move secret from the trustees. The town was moved about two miles from its original site. The community had better success in silk production than did Savannah. Some years they shipped more than 2,000 pounds of raw silk to England. It was such a good source of income that Ebenezer became known as the "Silk Capital." Ebenezer was controlled by the British during the Revolutionary War, but it was liberated by General Anthony Wayne in 1782. In the same year, the Georgia legislature met in the church.

***Jerusalem Church at New Ebenezer***

The Jerusalem Lutheran Church, begun in 1767 and completed in 1769, is the oldest standing church in Georgia. Atop the spire is a swan, the symbol of the Lutheran religion. Regular services have been held for more than 200 years. The town once boasted 500 citizens but the Revolutionary War brought bad times and by 1850, there were only two houses left in town. The old townsite is located in Effingham County, named in honor of the Earl of Effingham, an ardent supporter of colonial rights.

## Isle of Hope

### About 10 miles south of Savannah on Skidaway Road

*Isle of Hope Waterfront*

Noble Jones, John Fallowfield, and Henry Parker each received a land grant of 500 acres. Fallowfield was the assistant bailiff in the colony and his property was located between that of Jones and Parker. Fallowfield became a dissident and led a revolt against Oglethorpe. The revolt failed and Fallowfield was expelled and his land forfeited. Later, it was granted to Noble Jones, enabling him to expand his holdings beyond Wormsloe.

Parker was a cloth merchant and also served as bailiff for the colony. The area was originally named for him and called Parkersburg. It was changed to L'Ile d'Esperance (Isle of Hope) by royalists from France seeking refuge during the French Revolution.

## Midway

### 30 miles south of Savannah on U.S. Highway 17

*Midway Congregational Church*

Located in Liberty County (formerly St. John's Parish). Many think the name means midway between Savannah and the Altamaha River, the southern boundary of the original colony. However, the more accepted version is the name is derived from the Medway River in England. Over the years the spelling changed.

Across from historic Midway Church is a cemetery where Generals Daniel Stewart and James Screven are buried. Stewart was the great-grandfather of Theodore Roosevelt. Stewart County and Fort Stewart in Hinesville were named in his honor. Screven County and Fort Screven are named for General Screven.

Of special historic significance is the Midway Congregational Church which began in 1752. The fathers of Oliver Wendell Holmes, Chief Justice of the U.S. Supreme Court and Samuel B. Morse, inventor of the telegraph, were pastors of this church. In the first 111 years of its existence, the church produced two signers of the Declaration of Independence: Dr. Lyman Hall and Button Gwinnett, one U.S. Minister to a foreign country, six congressmen, four governors, 82 ministers, six foreign missionaries, two university chancellors, six professors, four authors, and miscellaneous scientists, teachers, attorneys, and physicians.

## Richmond Hill

### 15 miles south of Savannah on U.S. Highway 17

During the Civil War, Richmond Hill, then Ways Station, served as the final hurdle for General Sherman on his "March to the Sea." Here, he had to deal with Fort McAllister that had already successfully defended against seven assaults from the water by Union gunboats. The fort finally succumbed to a land assault by superior forces, thus removing the last impediment to Sherman's entry into Savannah.

In 1924 Richmond Hill witnessed a dramatic social and economic revolution under the guidance of Henry Ford. He purchased 85,000 acres in Bryan County, Ga., and erected "Ford Village," which encompassed 292 commercial and community buildings. Ford built schools, medical clinics, kindergartens, a church, a sawmill, and hundreds of homes. The entire area was renamed Richmond Hill, the same as Ford's winter home in the area.

## Thunderbolt

### Victory Drive and the Wilmington River

Named for a bolt of lightning that supposedly struck the area in Colonial times, shattering underlying rock and causing clear spring water to surface. The burning scent, created by the lightning, lingered at the spring for many years afterward.

Oglethorpe considered this area to be of strategic importance and built a fort to protect Savannah from Spanish attack. Soon Thunderbolt was serving as a point of embarkation for Frederica and other points south. During the siege of Savannah, Admiral D'Estaing, leader of the French allies, established his command post at Thunderbolt.

In 1856, an attempt was made to change the town's name to Warsaw, then the name of the Wilmington River, but the citizens favored the old name

*Waterfront at Thunderbolt*

and continued to use it. By 1875 it was home to a famous casino. At the time, gambling was legal in Georgia and was a drawing card at all the resort hotels. Thunderbolt was also home to the Yacht Club and the Jockey Club, with a racetrack nearby. By 1921, the town was finally incorporated, and officially recognized the popular name, "Thunderbolt."

## Tybee Island

### 15 miles east of Savannah on U.S. Highway 80

Tybee Island comprises five square miles. The name Tybee is interpreted as “salt” in the vocabulary of the Euchee Indians who originally inhabited the island. From early days, her shores have hosted the flags of Spain, England, France, the Confederacy, and sometimes even pirates.

In the nineteenth century the island served as a popular dueling spot for gentlemen from South Carolina. These encounters normally took place at the Martello Tower, a fortification erected by Isaiah Davenport, which would later become the site of Fort Screven at the northern end of the island.

In 1889, the Central of Georgia began a daily train from the city to the beach. The trip took about an hour. Then, in 1923, the highway was completed thus greatly diminishing the popularity of the railroad. The train was finally discontinued in 1933 but the old roadbed now serves as a nature walk and biker trail.

The island resort has always been popular with Savannahians and today has a stable year-round population. During the roaring twenties, many of the nationally known "big-name" dance bands played at Tybee on the Tybrisa pavilion.

# Memorable Events

## Dueling

Dueling was already outlawed in England when the colony of Georgia

***Aaron Burr - Alexander Hamilton Duel***

was founded. Although Oglethorpe's stance on dueling was never made public, it was felt he approved based on the way he handled the few cases appearing before him. As the colony grew, dueling became the way to satisfy disputes of any sort: property; personal injury; slander; a lady's virtue; and above all, honor.

The "Code Duello" became a sacred ritual, a dance of death, and a drama replete with unflinching participants. All this was accompanied by foolhardy seconds enforcing unwritten rules, attending surgeons, and spectators waiting in the wings. The press stood by, but reported little, in order to spare the grieving families. Usually only the death notices and funeral arrangements appeared in print. Finally, there was the clergy, rendered

*James Jackson*

helpless in the face of a code more powerful than the laws of God or man. This code was unique and sacred to Savannah people of all classes, who through the years had embellished it with romantic trappings of chivalry and legend. Southern gentlemen considered their reputation and honor paramount over any fatal consequence. Some of the more noted encounters were:

• Button Gwinnett v. Lachlan McIntosh - both were wounded in the leg. Gwinnett succumbed to a gangrene infection three days later.

• James Jackson v. many opponents - he was a short man with a short name and a short temper. While his enemies called him a brawling pigmy, his friends responded that he was tall in honesty, courage, and his love for Georgia. So violent was the Jackson temper, he didn't always wait for the slow formalities of the code. He would fight anyone, anytime, anywhere. Jackson was reputed to have survived 23 duels in his 49 years. Some of these were against the same opponent and most involved the promoters of the Yazoo Land Fraud in western Georgia.

• his first duel was against acting governor George Wells in 1780. He accused Wells of dishonesty and inordinate ambition. Wells was killed instantly.

• the next was against three time Savannah mayor, Thomas Gibbons, whom Jackson had charged with election falsifying when Jackson lost his bid for Congress to General Anthony Wayne. They exchanged three shots but neither man was hit. This is somewhat surprising since Gibbons supposedly weighed more than 350 pounds. Later, they became loyal friends and each went on to fame and fortune.

• three duels against Robert Watkins of the Yazoo Land interests. In the final duel, he wounded Watkins so severely, the seconds intervened. Jackson also suffered wounds that probably shortened his life.

• Nathanael Greene v. James Gunn - the dueling code was so entrenched in the Savannah mystique that even men of the highest reputation were reluctant to refuse a challenge for fear of being labeled a coward. This could be the slightest charge from the coarsest adversary. A notable exception was General Nathanael Greene. At the end of the Revolutionary War, when again a private citizen, Greene was challenged by Captain James Gunn, who was to become the mastermind of thc Yazoo Land Fraud. It seemed that Gunn, while serving under Greene, had been subjected to a congressional inquiry for selling a horse without orders. He received a reprimand. Greene refused the challenge saying if a superior officer could be held privately responsible for disciplining his men, all military regimen would be subverted.

Greene feared the loss of public esteem and wrote in anguish to George Washington for guidance. Washington agreed with his decision and replied that if a commanding officer is subject to private challenges for the discharge of his public duty, he will always have a dagger at his heart. Gunn again threatened Greene with a personal assault to which Greene coolly replied, "I always wear pistols and I will defend myself."

So what brought an end to dueling in Savannah? Not law, moral force, or outrage. Much of it was the wit of Joel Chandler Harris, creator of Uncle Remus, when he was a young reporter working for the Savannah Morning News. His recounting of the murderous clashes was so amusing that the principals became a laughing stock. And in Savannah, the proudest of all cities, ridicule was all that could eradicate the sacred code. No custom, no matter how time honored, could survive against derision, jeers, and laughter.

## Cotton Gin - 1793

Mulberry Grove was awarded to General Nathanael Greene by George Washington for his service to America during the Revolutionary War. He and his wife Caty moved there in 1785 but General Greene died within the year. Caty continued to live on the plantation.

Returning from Rhode Island, Caty met 27 year old Eli Whitney, a law student and recent graduate of Yale University. She invited him to Mulberry Grove while he awaited word regarding a teaching post in South Carolina. Whitney accepted her invitation expecting to only spend a few days there. Upon arriving, he learned the teaching job would pay much less than what he was told when recruited. Whitney declined the position but it left him stranded at Mulberry Grove with meager resources.

*Eli Whitney*

Mulberry Grove always had many guests and there was much talk about cotton from the visiting planters. They complained that raising cotton was difficult. Sea Island long staple cotton, where the seeds were easy to separate from the fiber, took longer for the crop to mature and produced only small bolls of cotton. Short staple cotton was the hardier crop but the seeds were hard to separate from the fiber. They knew if there was an efficient way of removing the seeds, it would create a profitable crop and much money could be made.

Caty had been impressed with Whitney's demonstrated mechanical ability in the short time he had been on the plantation. Apparently he had busied himself with repairing various equipment and even fixing her watch. She thought it would be interesting to see how Whitney's mechanical mind would approach the problem.

At Caty's request, Whitney closeted himself a few days before emerging and announcing that he thought he had the solution. Whitney's method was to use a comb that would separate the fiber from the seeds and then a brush revolving in the opposite direction to clean the teeth of the comb.

Phineas Miller, the plantation superintendent and tutor to the Greene children, immediately saw the potential of the new invention. Since Whitney had no money, Miller agreed to finance the development with a 50/50 split in profits.

Whitney went personally to Philadelphia to see the Secretary of State, an office then occupied by Thomas Jefferson. Jefferson was a tinkerer himself and he too saw the merit in Whitney's invention. He readily granted a patent on the cotton gin effective March 14, 1794.

Everyone got rich but Whitney. Although the gin was patented and marketed, it was too easy to duplicate and Whitney never made what he should on the invention. He sued but received little for his effort.

Prior to the cotton gin, slavery was waning. With efficient cotton processing, slavery was revived once more since the production of cotton required many laborers. Whitney had always been opposed to the institution of slavery and was disturbed at the prospect of its reawakening. Savannah became a boom town and a great port, setting world cotton prices and ultimately erecting the Savannah Cotton Exchange to "King Cotton."

The gin was Whitney's contribution to the South but his real gift to the country was the development of the mass production system. He is now regarded as the father of mass production in America. In 1798, the government awarded him a contract for 10,000 muskets which were to be delivered within two years. Previously, rifles had been crafted one at a time.

Whitney decided to cast the individual parts and make them interchangeable. This allowed their assembly later, in a process where great numbers could be turned out quickly. It was a novel idea receiving much skepticism, but Whitney prevailed. He even demonstrated his process for President John Adams by assembling a complete musket lock from randomly selected parts. The contract was delivered and mass production was born. Whitney died at the age of 59 years and is buried in New Haven, Connecticut.

At the outbreak of the Civil War, the Whitney process of mass production was turned on the South. Using this method, the North was producing 97 percent of all weapons manufactured in America at the time. Whitney had inadvertently continued the slavery he abhorred with the cotton gin, but now the process of mass production would seek his retribution.

## Downtown Fires

In 1796 fire began at the city market on Ellis Square when a stove overheated. Due to a lack of rain, the wooden buildings were very dry. Driven by a strong wind, the fire spread rapidly and soon destroyed more than 300 houses. The burned area spanned Bay Street to Oglethorpe Avenue and Barnard Street to Abercorn Street. This fire is one of the reasons Savannah has so few 18th century structures remaining.

Fire erupted again in 1820, this time on Franklin Square, only one block from the city market where the fire in 1796 began. This fire was said to be even worse since practically all structures north of Broughton Street, some 463 buildings, were lost. Again there had been a drought and again there was a strong wind. The result was a fire that raged across the city. It was one of the worst fires in American history.

***Fire at the Ammunition Depot in January 1865***

In January 1865, about a month after General Sherman occupied the city, fire broke out on the west side of town. More than 100 buildings were lost including the Confederate arsenal at the corner of West Broad Street (now Martin Luther King, Jr. Boulevard) and Broughton Street.

The last great fire started in 1889 at Hogan's Store at Barnard and Broughton Streets. Among the many buildings burned was the Independent Presbyterian Church at Bull Street and Oglethorpe Avenue. To guard against future fires, the city installed numerous giant cisterns at strategic locations.

## S.S. Savannah - 1819

Even from its early days, Savannah was an active shipbuilding site.

So it was only natural that several entrepreneurs, including William Scarbrough and Oliver Sturges, would back the venture for a trans-Atlantic steamship. In 1818 a stock issue was sold with Scarbrough being the largest investor. Sea captain Moses Rogers, a northerner knowledgeable in steamboats, purchased a boat called *Fickett's Steam Coffin* and had it modified and renamed the *S.S. Savannah*.

The *Savannah* was 110 feet in overall length with a beam of 25.8 feet and a draft of 13 feet. She was equipped with a 90-horsepower steam engine

***The S. S. Savannah - First Steamship to cross the Atlantic***

and boiler and also boasted three masts. The smokestack was fitted with an adjustable elbow to divert smoke and sparks away from the combustible sails.

President James Monroe and his Secretary of War, John C. Calhoun, were in Savannah as guests of William Scarbrough and took a trial excursion on the vessel to Tybee Island and back. To prove her worth and attract customers, the ship sailed across the Atlantic to Liverpool in only 29 days and 11 hours. As she approached the coast of Ireland, the cutter *Kite* chased the billowing smoke from the *Savannah,* thinking she was afire.

The *Savannah* bore into the port of Liverpool loaded with cotton from Oliver Sturges and dropped anchor. Although the ship generated a lot of curiosity, no commercial deals were struck. While in Europe, she visited ports in England, Ireland, Scotland, Sweden, and Russia. Eventually, she returned to America, being unable to interest commercial shippers in her practicality other than as a novelty.

The engine was sold and the ship placed in packet service. She was thought to be more serviceable without the steam engine since it took up space that could be devoted to cargo. After only a short service, the *Savannah* ran aground off Long Island, N.Y., November 5, 1821. The breakers in the surf destroyed her beyond salvage. The date of her initial departure across the Atlantic, May 22nd, is celebrated as National Maritime Day. Captain Moses Rogers is buried in the churchyard of St. David's Episcopal Church in Cheraw, South Carolina. William Scarbrough is buried in Colonial Park Cemetery.

## Gibbons versus Ogden

### U.S. Supreme Court Decision of 1824

The Robert Fulton Steamboat Company was granted a monopoly by the state of New York to operate on the waters within that state. Thomas Gibbons, three-time mayor of Savannah, began a rival steamship company, also operating on the waters within New York. The yet to be fabulously wealthy Cornelius Vanderbilt, the future "Commodore," was captain of one of Gibbons' boats. Gibbons' former partner, Aaron Ogden, now working for the Fulton company, became the defendant in the lawsuit filed by Gibbons to break the monopoly. Daniel Webster, one of the most respected attorneys of the day, was retained to represent Gibbons.

The lawsuit dragged on for years, finally arriving at the U.S. Supreme Court. Chief Justice John Marshall ruled that only the federal government had the right to regulate navigable waters in the United States. The monopoly was broken and Gibbons was victorious. The decision set a precedent which is now the basis of all law governing interstate commerce.

While in New York, Gibbons maintained his Savannah connections. It was probably his involvement in steamboats that sowed the seed resulting in the 1818 venture of the *S.S. Savannah*. Gibbons is buried in Elizabethtown, New Jersey.

## Lafayette's Visit

On March 19, 1825, the Marquis de Lafayette visited Savannah to dedicate a monument to his wartime friend, General Nathanael Greene. Lafayette and Greene were close comrades during the Revolutionary War and later, Greene's son was entrusted to Lafayette's care while completing his education in France.

*Marquis de Lafayette*

It had been 44 years since Lafayette, as a young French nobleman of 24 years, was at Yorktown assisting the Americans in their fight for independence.

The French king refused to grant Lafayette permission to support the American Revolution but he sailed anyway, purchasing and equipping a ship at his own expense. Continental Congress gave him a commission as a major general but primarily his duties were as aide-de-camp to General Washington.

To Washington he brought personal and political devotion with an eagerness and ability in the performance of military duties. He also brought the assurance that the Americans were not alone in their cause.

In 1781 he was given command of the defense of Virginia. His maneuvering eventually drew Charles Cornwallis, the English commander, into the trap at Yorktown. There, he was blockaded by both the French troops and American forces.

Lafayette was now 68 years of age. From the southern balcony of the Richardson-Owens-Thomas house, then a rooming house, he formally reviewed Savannah's militia as they paraded past. In addition to dedicating the monument to Greene, he placed a cornerstone for a future monument to Count Casimir Pulaski in Chippewa Square. He commented that it had been his honor to introduce Pulaski to General Washington. Lafayette laid five cornerstones for monuments during his return trip to America, two of those were in Savannah. He died in 1834. Fayette County was named in his honor.

## S.S. John Randolph

America's first successful iron steamboat used in commerce, was launched in the Savannah harbor July 9, 1834. It was named in honor of John Randolph of Virginia, a cousin of Thomas Jefferson. Randolph served four terms as a Congressman and one as a U.S. Senator. His brilliant justification of states' rights was the basis of argument that ultimately led the South to secede from the Union.

The idea of the iron ship was promoted and financed by Gazaway Bugg Lamar of Savannah, who was prominent in shipping and business circles. The boat was prefabricated in Birkenhead, England, shipped in segments, and assembled in Savannah. It was 100 feet in length with a 22-foot beam. Unlike the *S.S. Savannah*, it was an immediate success in the river trade. Being lighter in the water than wooden boats enabled it to successfully navigate the shallow waters between Savannah and Augusta.

It was the first of a great fleet of ironboats on the waterways of America. The boat was used as a blockade runner during the Civil War and was ultimately sunk off Sullivan's Island near Charleston in 1865. It was not recovered.

## The Last Slave Ship

C.A.L.(Charles Augustus Lafayette) Lamar, born April Fools Day, 1824, was the only surviving child of Gazaway B. Lamar, who launched the *S.S. John Randolph*. All six of his brothers and sisters, as well as his mother, perished in 1838 with the sinking of the steamship *Pulaski* off the coast of Charleston. The *Pulaski* was one of his father's ships that ran between Charleston and Savannah. His godfather and namesake was the Marquis de Lafayette, the French general and hero of the American Revolution. The Marquis was present at his christening while a visitor to the city in 1825.

Lamar was charged with managing the family business in Savannah and was very prominent in social circles. He was active in yachting and horse racing and served on the board of several banks and corporations. He was well respected, although argumentative and stubborn to a fault. Lamar engaged in several duels with men who rendered "imagined slights" to his honor. He had to be right, he could not compromise.

Lamar felt the federal laws concerning slavery were unconstitutional. They violated the right of an individual to buy whatever goods he desired and transport those goods to a destination of his own choosing. He even asked permission from Treasury Secretary Howell Cobb to bring slaves into the United States. Cobb refused. The importation of slaves had been banned in 1850.

Today, citizens are accustomed to legislation by government agency, but in the mid-nineteenth century, Lamar resented this unusual revocation of his rights. He said he had broken no law and even if he had, it was not up to the Treasury to punish him.

Lamar was fascinated with beautiful ships. He heard of the sleekness and speed of the ship *Wanderer,* built for a wealthy New Yorker, and was

***The Slaveship Wanderer***

determined to possess it. He and some friends traveled to New York, bought the boat, and sailed to Charleston where they secretly outfitted it as a slave ship.

Lamar's father took a dim view of his scheme. In a letter to him he said, "An expedition to the moon would have been equally sensible and no more contrary to the laws of Providence. May God forgive you for all your attempts to violate his will and his laws."

***James Moore Wayne***

In the spring of 1859, Lamar sailed to Africa on the *Wanderer* with John Farnum along as captain. There, they purchased 750 slaves and returned to a deserted beach on Jekyll Island, Georgia, where the slaves were disbursed to various plantations in small boats. Eighty of the slaves succumbed during the passage.

Upon learning of this violation, the U.S. District Attorney in Savannah seized the *Wanderer* and arrested Lamar, Farnum, and others involved. Lamar resided in sumptuous quarters in his apartment while a jury was stacked with 18 Savannahians. The case was tried before Supreme Court Justice James Moore Wayne and prosecuted by Henry R. Jackson, both of Savannah, in the U.S. Custom House, also in Savannah.

Lamar's trial and "private incarceration" became a local festival. He stole the keys to Farnum's cell in the city jail and released him to party in his more comfortable quarters on Bay Street.

Lamar and all involved, including his friend Carey Styles, mayor of Brunswick and later founder of the *Atlanta Constitution*, were acquitted of major charges. Apparently the stacked jury felt the federal government had no right to interfere with the "rights" of a citizen of a state. Lamar and Styles each received a $500 dollar fine and 30 days confinement, which they served in Lamar's apartment, above his office.

At the outbreak of the Civil War, Captain Farnum was commissioned a major in the New York Volunteers and served with such gallantry that he was promoted to brigadier general. Apparently being active in the slave trade, just before fighting to abolish it, did not bother Farnum. Lamar served with the Confederacy and was captured on April 16, 1865, in a battle near Columbus, Georgia. At the time he was serving as an aide to his cousin, General Howell Cobb. Lamar died when the men in blue, thinking he was reaching for a gun, reacted quickly and fired at him. As a result, the nation's last slave trader is often listed as the last combat casualty of the Civil War. Lamar is buried in Laurel Grove Cemetery very close to Judge Wayne and under his watchful eye.

## Slavery

Early regulations in the colony outlawed slavery and prohibited land holdings of more than 50 acres. The purpose was to avoid the plantation system of neighboring South Carolina. Even though slavery was permitted beginning 1751, Georgia outlawed foreign slave trade in the constitution of 1798. However, the measure was often circumvented and finally repealed in 1824.

***Bidding for Human Lives***

Although there was never an active slave market in Savannah, one of the largest slave auctions to take place in Georgia was when Pierce Butler sold 460 slaves here.

As General Sherman's army neared the city in December 1864, many ads appeared in the Savannah newspaper as nervous, optimistic owners made a final attempt to sell their slaves before they were liberated.

## Evacuation of Savannah

General Sherman's Union army of 60,000 closed in on Savannah in December 1864. General William Hardee, commanding a small Confederate force of about 10,000, made plans to elude Sherman through a back door escape hatch into South Carolina. Pontoon type bridges were laid by troops from the Confederate navy and the Georgia militia. Large cotton flats were used as boats, railroad wheels were used as anchors, and planks from the city wharves were used as flooring. The first bridge began from the foot of West Broad Street (Martin Luther King, Jr. Boulevard) and extended to Hutchinson

*Evacuation of Savannah*

Island. Once there, another spanned the Back River to Pennyworth Island while a final bridge crossed the Little Back River to the Carolina shore.

The troops from Whitemarsh Island were drawn back into the city to be evacuated via the bridges. At dark on the 20th of December the garrisons of Causton Bluff, Thunderbolt, and the Savannah River batteries, gathered at Fort Jackson to be transferred by steamer to Screven's Ferry (across the river near the present Talmadge Bridge). The main garrison of infantry, cavalry, light artillery and wagons, crossed on the pontoon bridges. They even covered the bridges with rice to muffle the sounds of their hasty departure. Well before dawn, the last of the rear guard cleared Hutchinson Island. When all the troops were on the other side and safely marching to Hardeeville, the end of the bridge anchored to the Savannah side was cut adrift.

*William Hardee*

Sherman's capture of Savannah included 25,000 bales of cotton which were of great monetary value. The Confederate House of Representatives and President Jefferson Davis demanded an answer from General Hardee as to why the cotton was not destroyed by the retreating Confederate army.

The answer was both simple and logical. Although a large portion of the cotton was on the wharf, much of it was disbursed throughout the city in cellars, garrets, and warehouses and could not have been burned without destroying the city. Also, all available manpower was assigned the more important task of completing the pontoon bridge to South Carolina.

After the war, General Ulysses S. Grant, who had commanded all

*Cotton on the Wharf in Savannah*

Union forces, took much enjoyment in needling Sherman about Hardee's escape. Many military observers considered the move to be brilliant. Perhaps Hardee's escape was taken right out of his own book.

Interestingly, the standard military textbook for both the North and the South during the war was, "*Rifle and Light Infantry Tactics,*" by William Hardee. It was referred to on both sides as "Hardee's Tactics." The text was written in 1856 at the time Hardee had served as commandant at West Point. Although he lived in Savannah for a few years both before and after the war, Hardee is buried in Selma, Alabama. There is a marker noting the evacuation on the north side of Bay Street between Jefferson and Barnard Streets.

## Development of Wesson Oil

Dr. David Wesson's name is well known today and identified with the cooking oil he developed. What is not well known is that his laboratory was in Savannah while he was an employee of the Southern Cotton Oil Company. In 1899 he discovered a process for making a vegetable based cooking oil from soybeans that led to the production of Wesson Oil and Snowdrift solid shortening. He also did extensive work in developing the protein in cottonseed meal for human consumption.

## Auto Racing

These races were sponsored by the Automobile Club of America. They began in 1908 with the American Grand Prize Race and ended with the Vanderbilt Cup in 1911. They even predated the Indianapolis 500, which ran its inaugural race in 1911. In 1908, 22 cars were entered representing four nations. The race was won by Louis Wagner at a speed of 65.08 mph. One driver with name recognition, Louis Chevrolet, made it his last race before he retired and devoted his efforts to designing and engineering the cars that would bear his name. Another American car buff, who attended largely unnoticed but played a large role in later Savannah history, was Henry Ford of Michigan. More than 100,000 spectators came to Savannah to witness the races.

The starting line was on Victory Drive at Waters Avenue. Spectator stands were erected on both sides of the street. From there the course ran west to Bull Street; south to Montgomery Crossroads; east to Waters Avenue; north to Eisenhower Road; east to Sally Mood Road; south to Montgomery Crossroads; west to Whitefield Avenue; south to Shipyard Road; east to Ferguson Avenue; north to Skidaway Road; south to Isle of Hope; east to LaRoche; north to the Shell Road; east to Thunderbolt and the waterfront; and west on Victory Drive to the finish line at Waters Avenue. The course was 25.13 miles long and required 16 laps to complete the 402.18 mile race.

***Racing for the Grand Prize in Savannah***

In 1909, due to fatalities on a course on Long Island, the race in Savannah was canceled. In 1910 the Grand Prize Race was held again in Savannah. A driver in that race, whose family would eventually settle in Savannah, was Washington Roebling II. He finished second in a Mercer that was manufactured by his family in Trenton, New Jersey. Roebling's namesake was the builder of the Brooklyn Bridge in New York City. Roebling II was aboard the Titanic when she went down in the Atlantic in 1912.

Both the Grand Prize Race in 1910 and the Vanderbilt Cup in 1911 were won by David Bruce-Brown. The following year he was killed in a Milwaukee race driving the same Fiat that was victorious in Savannah.

With the increase in auto traffic on the streets, inconvenience, and cost in time and money, the races were discontinued. Their legacy was that they were referred to by those who knew road racing as, "the greatest ever held in America."

In 1997, racing again came to Savannah with the running of the Indy Lights on the new course on Hutchinson Island.

## The Southern Paper Industry

Charles Holmes Herty was born in Milledgeville in 1867. He graduated from the University of Georgia and remained there as a professor. Chemistry and sports were his primary interests. During his tenure, he organized and coached Georgia's first football team and the playing field in Athens was named in his honor.

Herty moved to Savannah in 1932 during the depth of the depression. He was 60 years old. It was generally thought at the time that pine trees were too resinous to produce white paper. Herty knew better. Turpentine and resin were products of tree wounds and not a natural component of healthy pines. He was convinced that pines could be used for newsprint.

*Charles Holmes Herty*

In 1933, nine Georgia newspapers tested the newsprint he developed from slash pine. The results were more than convincing and it didn't take long for paper plants to begin moving south. The discovery was a tremendous financial boon to the South as it struggled to emerge from the Great Depression.

Union Camp opened a large plant in Savannah in 1936 and has provided jobs for thousands since. By 1937, 13 paper plants were operating in the South. Herty died in Savannah in 1938. He was cremated and his ashes interred in Macon. Herty Foundation in Savannah continues his research.

## International Monetary Conference

The International Monetary Conference met in Savannah following the Bretton Woods Conference in 1945. It was hosted by the General Oglethorpe Hotel (now the Sheraton) on Wilmington Island in March 1946. The conference was instrumental in setting the parity of the dollar to gold until America left the gold standard many years later. Among the notables in attendance were the British economist Lord John Maynard Keynes and Lady Nancy Astor. Lady Astor had commented during an earlier visit that "Savannah was like a pretty woman with a dirty face." The remark embarrassed the city but also awakened it as to how it was viewed by outsiders.

## St. Patrick's Day

Celebrated in Savannah since the early 1800's. Today, the St. Patrick's Day parade is the second largest in the country trailing only New York City. Savannahians often say, tongue-in-cheek, that their parade is second largest and New York's is second best. The celebration is the third oldest in the country, only behind New York City and Boston.

# Museums

## The Beach Institute

**Price and Harris Streets**

The Beach Institute was established in 1865 as a school for black children. It was named for Alfred E. Beach, philanthropist and editor of Scientific American magazine. Teachers were sent to Savannah from the northern American Missionary Association. Today, the Beach Institute is a museum where a rich variety of African American cultural programs can be seen.

## Central of Georgia Railroad Complex

**Martin Luther King, Jr. Boulevard and Liberty Street**

***Central of Georgia Railway Roundhouse***

In 1834 a study was commissioned to determine the feasibility of building a railroad to the interior of the state. The report not only concluded it was feasible but highly recommended. William Washington Gordon, then mayor of Savannah, was very involved in the railroad's development. He was a heavy investor and became the first president of the Central Railway and Banking Company, chartered in 1835. The 190 miles of track to Macon made it the longest railroad in America owned by a single company.

With other investors, the city subscribed to 5,000 shares of stock and donated five acres of land west of the intersection of Martin Luther King, Jr. Boulevard and Liberty Street. It included the provision that the land would revert to the city if no longer used by the railroad. After 136 years of operations, this came to pass. In 1971, when the last train passed through the station, the land reverted back to the city. It now houses the Chamber of Commerce Visitors Center and Savannah History Museum.

The brick Gothic Revival guard towers at the entrance were erected to secure a gate and stand guard over the large rail yard. The area once boasted three miles of tracks and platforms and held up to 20,000 bales of cotton at one time.

Construction of the repair shops began in 1845 and is an excellent example of 19th century railroad manufacturing and repair facilities. Thirteen of the original structures are still standing, including the 125-foot brick smokestack, roundhouse, and turntable. It is considered to be the most complete antebellum railroad structure surviving in the country today. The site is a National Historic Landmark. It offers many interesting displays. The shops are open to the public and are operated by the Coastal Heritage Society.

## Ralph Mark Gilbert Civil Rights Museum

### Martin Luther King, Jr. Boulevard and Alice Street

Showcases Savannah's role in the civil rights movement. The museum is housed in the old Guaranty Life Insurance building. This location became the headquarters of the Savannah branch of the NAACP movement that directed the freedom struggle. Dr. Ralph Mark Gilbert was considered by many to be the pioneer of the civil rights movement in Savannah. He was the pastor of the First African Baptist Church and lead the local chapter of the NAACP from 1942-1950. He was also a leader in educational, civic, and human rights activities until his death in 1956. He is buried in the Lincoln Memorial Cemetery at Hunter Field in Savannah. His papers and memorabilia are on exhibit at the museum. Open to the public.

## King-Tisdell Cottage
### 514 E. Huntingdon Street

The small Victorian cottage was built in 1896 for W.W. Aimer. The cottage is significant for its intricate gingerbread ornamentation on the porch and dormers in a style employing wheels and spindles. It was purchased in 1910 by Eugene King, a black businessman. After his death, his widow married Robert Tisdell.

*King-Tisdell Cottage*

The structure is a center for learning and showcasing black history. It is operated as a museum by the Savannah Yamacraw Chapter of the Association for the Study of Afro-American Life and History. The museum displays art objects and documents relating to black history and furniture appropriate to a coastal black residence of the 1890's. The cottage is open to the public.

## Mighty Eighth Air Force Heritage Museum
### Intersection of I-95 and U.S. 80 West

The Eighth Air Force was formed in Savannah at the National Guard Armory on Bull Street and Park Avenue in January 1942 and immediately deployed to the United Kingdom. Some 350,000 men and women served during WWII with about one half of those being combat crew members. The Eighth became the largest air force in the history of aviation. The cost in casualties was awesome. Of an estimated 200,000 combat crew personnel, 26,000 were killed, 28,000 were captured, and 9,000 planes were lost to enemy fire. The museum tells the story of the Eighth's commitment, challenge, and courage. It honors the more than one million men and women who have served in the Eighth since 1942. Open to the public.

## Oatland Island Education Center

### About six miles east of town on Islands Expressway

Features 60 acres of nature trails and a heritage site with 19th century period cabins. Many endangered species of Georgia can be seen, e.g., eagles, panthers, wolves, eastern woods bison, and alligators. Also very popular is the Delk-Dawson farm, centered around a log cabin originally built in 1835. Here, activities designed to illustrate life on a small south Georgia farm of the period provide a living history experience. On some weekends there are demonstrations of cane grinding, weaving, sheep shearing, candle making, and other skills that are performed by costumed craftsmen at the farm. Open to the public.

## River Street Train Museum

### 315 W. River Street

For the model railroading enthusiast. It features a nostalgic operating layout and miniature town. Also presented are toy train displays, from the 1930's to current production models, and other railroad memorabilia. Many models are available for sale in the gift shop.

## Savannah History Museum

### Martin Luther King, Jr. Boulevard and Liberty Street

This building, housing the History Museum and the Visitors Center, was constructed in 1861 as a passenger terminal for the Central of Georgia Railway. The Savannah gray bricks used in the structure were fired at the Hermitage Plantation on the Savannah River. The last train departing from this terminal was on April 30, 1971.

Two theaters and an exhibit hall graphically portray the Battle of

*Central of Georgia Railway Passenger Terminal*

Savannah fought on this site in October 1779. Items of interest on display include a 1890 Central of Georgia locomotive and a working cotton gin. Exhibited are flags and uniforms from America's military history beginning with the Revolutionary War and extending through American involvement in Vietnam.

Forrest Gump's bench, from the movie of the same name, is here. Also displayed is a replica of the "Bird Girl" statue featured on the cover of the book *"Midnight in the Garden of Good and Evil."* Open to the public. Most of the historic bus tours originate from this location.

## Ships of the Sea Maritime Museum

### Martin Luther King, Jr. Boulevard and Congress Street

Located in the Scarbrough House, the museum contains historic displays of ship models and other nautical memorabilia. Among the collection is General Oglethorpe's Anne, the ship that brought the original colonists to Georgia; The S.S. Savannah, the first steamship to cross the Atlantic; H.M.S. Rose, the British ship that was scuttled in the Savannah River during the siege of 1779; Columbus's Santa Maria; a sinking Titanic, and many others.

Authentic figureheads are scattered throughout the museum. Early naval weapons, a shipboard surgeon's kit and a sailor's mess kit are woven into the nautical theme. In the basement is a life-sized replica of a ship's wheelhouse. Open to the public.

## Skidaway Marine Science Complex
### Skidaway Island

The aquarium exhibits live specimens of marine life found in the coastal area including an excellent array of salt water fish. The institute conducts ongoing research aboard its own 72-foot research vessel and is affiliated with the University of Georgia. Open to the public.

## Tybee Island Marine Science Center
### 1510 Strand at 14th Street

The center offers visitors unique opportunities to learn about the amazing assortment of marine life in our local environment. Featured are aquariums containing species indigenous to the coast of south Georgia. It also offers a small library, video room, a cross section of the beach, and exhibits featuring sharks, shells, marine mammals and marine pollution. Open to the public.

## Tybee Island Lighthouse and Museum
### Fort Screven across from Lighthouse

The museum offers an insightful portrait into the history and color of the island. It features archival photographs and artifacts from the early days on the island's historic shores. Open to the public.

## At Rest

| | |
|---|---|
| Aiken, Conrad | Bonaventure Cemetery |
| Anderson, Major George W. | Laurel Grove Cemetery |
| Armstrong, George Ferguson | Bonaventure Cemetery |
| Asendorff, Cord | Bonaventure Cemetery |
| Bartow, General Francis S. | Laurel Grove Cemetery |
| Berrien, John MacPherson | Laurel Grove Cemetery |
| Bosomworth, Reverend Thomas | St. Catherine's Island, Georgia |
| Bowen, Oliver | St. Paul's Churchyard - Augusta |
| Bryan, Jonathan | Brampton Plantation |
| Bryan, Reverend Andrew | Laurel Grove Cemetery - South |
| Bull, William | Sheldon Plantation, S.C. |
| Bulloch, Archibald | Colonial Park Cemetery |
| Champion, Aaron | Laurel Grove Cemetery |
| Charlton, Mayor Thomas U.P. | Laurel Grove Cemetery |
| Cottineau, Captain Denis L. | Colonial Park Cemetery |
| Crawford, William Harris | Crawford, Georgia |
| Davenport, Isaiah | Unknown |
| Elbert, Samuel | Colonial Park Cemetery |
| Elliot, Bishop Stephen | Laurel Grove Cemetery |
| Ellis, Governor Henry | Naples, Italy |
| Estill, John H. | Bonaventure Cemetery |
| Forsyth, Governor John | Congressional Cemetery - Wash., D.C. |
| Gallie, Major John B. | Laurel Grove Cemetery |
| Gaston, William | Bonaventure Cemetery |
| Gibbons, Thomas | Elizabethtown, N.J. |
| Gilbert, Reverend Ralph Mark | Lincoln Memorial - Hunter Field |
| Gilmer, General Jeremy F. | Laurel Grove Cemetery |
| Gordon, General John B. | Oakland Cemetery - Atlanta |
| Gordon, Nellie Kinzie | Laurel Grove Cemetery |

| | |
|---|---|
| Gordon, William Washington | St. Paul's Churchyard - Augusta |
| Gordon, William Washington II | Laurel Grove Cemetery |
| Green, Charles | Greenwich, Virginia |
| Greene, Caty | Cumberland Island, Georgia |
| Greene, General Nathanael | Johnson Square |
| Gwinnett, Button | Colonial Park Cemetery |
| Habersham, James | Colonial Park Cemetery |
| Habersham, James, Jr. | Colonial Park Cemetery |
| Habersham, John | Colonial Park Cemetery |
| Habersham, Joseph | Colonial Park Cemetery |
| Hall, Dr. Lyman | Independence Shrine in Augusta |
| Hardee, General William | Selma, Alabama |
| Harrison, General Paul J. | Laurel Grove Cemetery |
| Herty, Dr. Charles Holmes | Macon, Georgia |
| Hodgson, Margaret Telfair | Bonaventure Cemetery |
| Hodgson, William B. | Bonaventure Cemetery |
| Houstoun, John | Estate at White Bluff - Savannah |
| Hunter, General Frank O'Driscoll | Laurel Grove Cemetery |
| Jackson, General Henry Rootes | Bonaventure Cemetery |
| Jackson, James | Congressional Cemetery - Wash., D.C. |
| Jasper, Sergeant William | Siege of Savannah Battlefield |
| Jay, William | Island of Mauritius - Indian Ocean |
| Jones, Noble | Bonaventure Cemetery |
| Jones, Noble Wimberly | Bonaventure Cemetery |
| Lafayette, The Marquis de | Paris, France |
| Lamar, Charles Augustus Lafayette | Laurel Grove Cemetery |
| Lamar, Gazaway Bugg | Alexandria, Virginia |
| Lawton, General Alexander Robert | Bonaventure Cemetery |
| Leile, Reverend George | Jamaica |
| Low, Andrew | Laurel Grove Cemetery |
| Low, Juliette Gordon | Laurel Grove Cemetery |

| | |
|---|---|
| Maitland, Colonel John | Haddington, Scotland |
| Marshall, Mary | Laurel Grove Cemetery |
| Marshall, Reverend Andrew Cox | Laurel Grove Cemetery - South |
| Martus, Florence | Laurel Grove Cemetery |
| McAlpin, Henry | Laurel Grove Cemetery |
| McGlashan, General Peter | Laurel Grove Cemetery |
| McIntosh, General Lachlan | Colonial Park Cemetery |
| McLaws, General Lafayette | Laurel Grove Cemetery |
| Meldrim, Peter W. | Bonaventure Cemetery |
| Mercer, General Hugh Weedon | Bonaventure Cemetery |
| Mercer, Johnny | Bonaventure Cemetery |
| Milledge, John | Summerville, Georgia |
| Miller, Phineas | Cumberland Island, Georgia |
| Mulryne, Colonel John | Nassau - Bahamas |
| Musgrove, Mary | St. Catherine's Island, Georgia |
| Newton, Sergeant John | Buried at sea |
| Oglethorpe, James Edward | Cranham, England |
| Olmstead, Colonel Charles H. | Laurel Grove Cemetery |
| O'Connor, Flannery | Milledgeville, Georgia |
| Pierpont, James Lord | Laurel Grove Cemetery |
| Pitt, William - Earl of Chatham | Westminster Abbey - London |
| Pulaski, Count Casimir | At Sea or Monterey Square |
| Rogers, Captain Moses | St. David's Church - Cheraw, S.C. |
| Scarbrough, William | Colonial Park Cemetery |
| Screven, General James | Midway Congregational Cemetery |
| Sheftall, Sheftall "Cocked Hat" | Sheftall Cemetery |
| Sherman, General William T. | St. Louis, Missouri |
| Smets, Alexander | Laurel Grove Cemetery |
| Sorrel, Francis | Laurel Grove Cemetery |
| Sorrel, General G. Moxley | Laurel Grove Cemetery |
| Stewart, General Daniel | Midway Congregational Cemetery |

| | |
|---|---|
| Tattnall, Josiah | England |
| Tattnall, Josiah Jr. | Bonaventure Cemetery |
| Tattnall, Josiah III | Bonaventure Cemetery |
| Tefft, Israel | Laurel Grove Cemetery |
| Telfair, Alexander | Winchester, Virginia |
| Telfair, Edward | Bonaventure Cemetery |
| Telfair, Mary | Bonaventure Cemetery |
| Thomas, Margaret | Laurel Grove Cemetery |
| Tomochichi | Wright Square |
| Tondee, Peter | Colonial Park Cemetery |
| Troup, Governor George Michael | Laurens County, Georgia |
| Walton, George | Independence Shrine in Augusta |
| Watson, Little Gracie | Bonaventure Cemetery |
| Wayne, General Anthony | Erie, Pennsylvania |
| Wayne, General Henry C. | Laurel Grove Cemetery |
| Wayne, James Moore | Laurel Grove Cemetery |
| Weed, Henry D. | Laurel Grove Cemetery |
| Wesley, Reverend Charles | Mary Lebone Parish Church - London |
| Wesley, Reverend John | City Road Chapel - London |
| Whitefield, Reverend George | Newburyport, Massachusetts |
| Whitney, Eli | New Haven, Connecticut |
| Willis, General Edward C. | Richmond, Virginia |
| Wiltberger, Peter | Bonaventure Cemetery |
| Wright, Governor James | Westminster Abbey - London |

# References


Abodaher, David J., *"Freedom Fighter: Casimir Pulaski,"* Julian Messner, 1969.

Adams, James Mack, *"A History of Fort Screven Georgia,"* JMA2 Publications, 1996.

Albu, Susan H. & Elizabeth Arndt, *"Here's Savannah: A Journey through Historic Savannah & Environs,"* 1994.

Barrow, Elfrida DeRenne and Laura Palmer Bell, *"Anchored Yesterdays: The Logbook of Savannah's Voyage Across A Georgia Century; In Ten Watches,"* The Review Publishing and Printing Company in the City of Savannah, 1923.

Bartley, Numan V., *"The Creation of Modern Georgia,"* The University of Georgia Press, 1983.

Bell, Malcolm, Jr., *"Savannah, Ahoy!"* The Pigeonhole Press, 1959.

Boyd, Kenneth W., *"Georgia Historical Markers - Coastal Counties,"* Cherokee Publishing Company, 1991.

Braynard, Frank O., *"S.S. Savannah: The Elegant Steam Ship,"* Dover Publications, Inc., 1963.

Capps, Clifford Sheats and Eugenia Burney, *"Colonial Georgia,"* Thomas Nelson, Inc., 1972.

Coleman, Kenneth and Charles Stephen Gurr, *"Dictionary of Georgia Biography,"* University of Georgia Press, 1983.

Coulter, E. Merton, Editor, *"The Journal of Peter Gordon,"* University of Georgia Press, 1963.

Conner, Tim, *"Savannah: Guidebook for the Eighties,"* Colonial Press, Inc., 1985.

Cooper, Emmeline King and Polly Wylly Cooper, *"A Visitor's Guide to Savannah,"* Wyrick & Company, 1995.

DeBolt, Margaret Wayt, *"Savannah: A Historical Portrait,"* The Donning Company, 1976.

DeBolt, Margaret Wayt, *"Savannah Specters,"* The Donning Company, 1984.

Fancher, Betsy, *"Savannah: A Renaissance of the Heart,"* Doubleday and Company, Inc., 1976.

Gamble, Thomas, *"Savannah Duels and Duelists,"* Review Publishing & Printing Company, 1923.

Gamble, Thomas, *"Savannah Monuments,"* Savannah Public Library, Georgia Historical Collection.

Garrison, Webb, *"A Treasury of Georgia Tales,"* Rutledge Hill Press, 1987.

Granger, Mary, Editor, *"Savannah River Plantations,"* The Georgia Historical Society, 1947.

Harden, William, *"A History of Savannah and South Georgia,"* Cherokee Publishing Company, 1981.

Johnson, Alan and Dumas Malone, Editors, *"Dictionary of American Biography,"* Scribner and Sons, 1929.

Johnson, James M., *"Militiamen, Rangers, and Redcoats: The Military in Georgia, 1754-1776,"* Mercer University Press, 1992.

Jones, George Fenwick, *"The Georgia Dutch,"* The University of Georgia Press, 1992.

Killion, Ronald G. and Charles D. Waller, *"Georgia and the Revolution,"* Cherokee Publishing Company, 1975.

Klein, Marilyn W. and David P. Fogle, *"Clues to American Architecture,"* Starhill Press, 1985.

Knight, Lucian Lamar, *"A Standard History of Georgia and Georgians,"* The Lewis Publishing Company, 1917.

Lane, Mills, *"Savannah Revisited: A Pictorial History,"* The Beehive Press, 1969.

Lane, Mills, *"The People of Georgia,"* The Beehive Press, 1992.

Lawrence, Alexander A., *"Storm Over Savannah,"* University of Georgia Press, 1951.

Lawrence, Alexander A., *"A Present for Mr. Lincoln,"* The Ardivan Press, 1961.

Levy, B.H., *"Savannah's Old Jewish Community Cemeteries,"* Mercer University Press, 1983.

Meldrim, Mrs. Peter W., *"An Historic Pilgrimage Through Savannah and Some of Its Environs,"* The Colonial Dames, 1921.

Nevin, David and the Editors of Time-Life Books, *"Sherman's March: Atlanta to the Sea,"* Time-Life Books, 1986.

Nichols, Frederick D. and Van Jones Martin, *"The Architecture of Georgia,"* The Beehive Press, 1976.

Northen, William J., *"Men of Mark in Georgia,"* A.B. Caldwell Publisher, 1907.

Patzl-Traub, Dr. Ulrike, *"Sojourn in Savannah,"* 1995.

Quattlebaum, Julian K., M.D., *"The Great Savannah Races: 1908, 1910, 1911,"* The R.L. Bryan Co., 1957.

Rhyne, Nancy, *"Touring the Coastal Georgia Backroads,"* R.R. Donnelley & Sons, 1994.

Rice, Bradley R. and Harvey H. Jackson, *"Georgia: The Empire State of the South,"* Windsor Publications, Inc., 1988.

Russell, Preston and Barbara Hines, *"Savannah: A History of Her People Since 1733,"* Frederic C. Beil, Publisher, 1992.

Scruggs, Carroll Proctor, *"Georgia During the Revolution,"* Bay Tree Grove Publishers, 1975.

Sieg, Edward Chan, *"The Squares: An Introduction to Savannah,"* The Donning Company Publishers, 1984.

Sieg, Edward Chan, *"Eden On the Marsh: An Illustrated History of Savannah,"* Windsor Publications, Inc., 1985.

Spector, Tom, *"The Guide to the Architecture of Georgia,"* University of South Carolina Press, 1993.

Spitler, Rita F., *"Higher Ground: Historic Churches and Synagogues in Savannah,"* 1995.

Stewart, Dorothy H., *"The Monuments and Fountains of Savannah,"* Armstong State College, Savannah, June 1993.

Stokes, Thomas L., *"The Savannah,"* Rinehart & Co., Inc., 1951.

Toledano, Roiulhac, *"The National Trust Guide to Savannah: Architectural & Cultural Treasures,"* John Wiley & Sons, Inc., 1997.

# Illustration Credits

Library of Congress
- General William T. Sherman
- View of Savannah in 1734 by colonist Peter Gordon
- Richardson-Owens-Thomas House

Georgia Historical Society
- Charles Herty
- Henry McAlpin
- Old City Market
- Wayne-Gordon House
- *S.S. Savannah*
- Savannah in 1837 by Fermin Cerveau

Chatham-Effingham-Liberty Regional Library (Gamble Collection)
- The Cotton Gin
- Nathanael Greene
- James Habersham
- William Hardee
- James Jackson
- Lachlan McIntosh
- The British Defense Line Marker
- The *Wanderer*
- Storming Fort McAllister
- Grand Prize Auto Racing
- Anthony Wayne
- Eli Whitney

Chatham-Effingham-Liberty Regional Library (Olmstead Collection)
- Champion-McAlpin House

New York Historical Society - Pierre Havens
- Slaves picking cotton outside Savannah in 1850's
- Cotton on the Wharf in Savannah

Fort Pulaski National Monument
- Charles d' Estaing
- Charles H. Olmstead
- Fort Pulaski
- James Wright

## Illustration Credits

H. Paul Blatner

Robert E. Lee and Joseph E. Johnston
Tomochichi and Toonahowi

Margaret Prevost Wood

Augustine Prevost

Historical Collections of Georgia - George White

Sheftall "Cocked Hat" Sheftall
George Michael Troup
George Whitefield

V. and J. Duncan Antique Maps and Prints

The Gwinnett-McIntosh Duel
The Burr-Hamilton Duel
Lady Nancy Astor (from the Ladies Home Journal)
The Marquis de Lafayette
Benjamin Lincoln
William Pitt
The Pulaski Monument
James Moore Wayne
Charles Wesley

Savannah News-Press

Frank O'Driscoll Hunter
Johnny Mercer
Clarence Thomas

Georgia Department of Community Development - Tourist Division

Fort Frederica

Juliette Gordon Low Girl Scout National Center

Nellie Gordon
Juliette Gordon Low

Georgia Department of Archives and History

Casimir Pulaski
William Scarbrough
Siege of Savannah

Duke University - Manuscript Department (William R. Perkins Library)

The Hermitage Plantation

Collection of Jay P. Altmayer

The Slave Auction

## Illustration Credits

Beincke Rare Book & Manuscript Library - Yale University
- John C. Calhoun

Frank and Marie T. Wood Print Collections
- Bidding for Human Lives
- Evacuation of Savannah
- Explosion of C.S.S. Savannah
- Citizens for Food
- Fire in 1865

University of Georgia Library - Special Collections
- Archibald Bulloch
- Early Georgia Inhabitants
- The Filature House
- Button Gwinnett
- Joseph Habersham
- Lyman Hall
- John Houstoun
- The Liberty Boys
- James Edward Oglethorpe
- Oglethorpe Greets the Indians
- Vanderbilt Race Poster
- George Walton

Higher Ground - Rita Spitler
- Independent Presbyterian Church
- Lutheran Church of the Ascension
- St. John's Episcopal Church
- Unitarian Universalist Church
- Wesley Monumental United Methodist Church

National Archives
- General John Gordon

Telfair Museum of Art
- Caty Greene
- Mary Telfair

Harper's Weekly
- Franklin Square
- The Peanut Lady
- Savannah Houses on Factor's Walk
- Savannah River Scene - 1872

# Illustration Credits

Chris Frederman

Bethesda Orphanage

The Countess of Huntingdon

# Index

# Historic Area Map

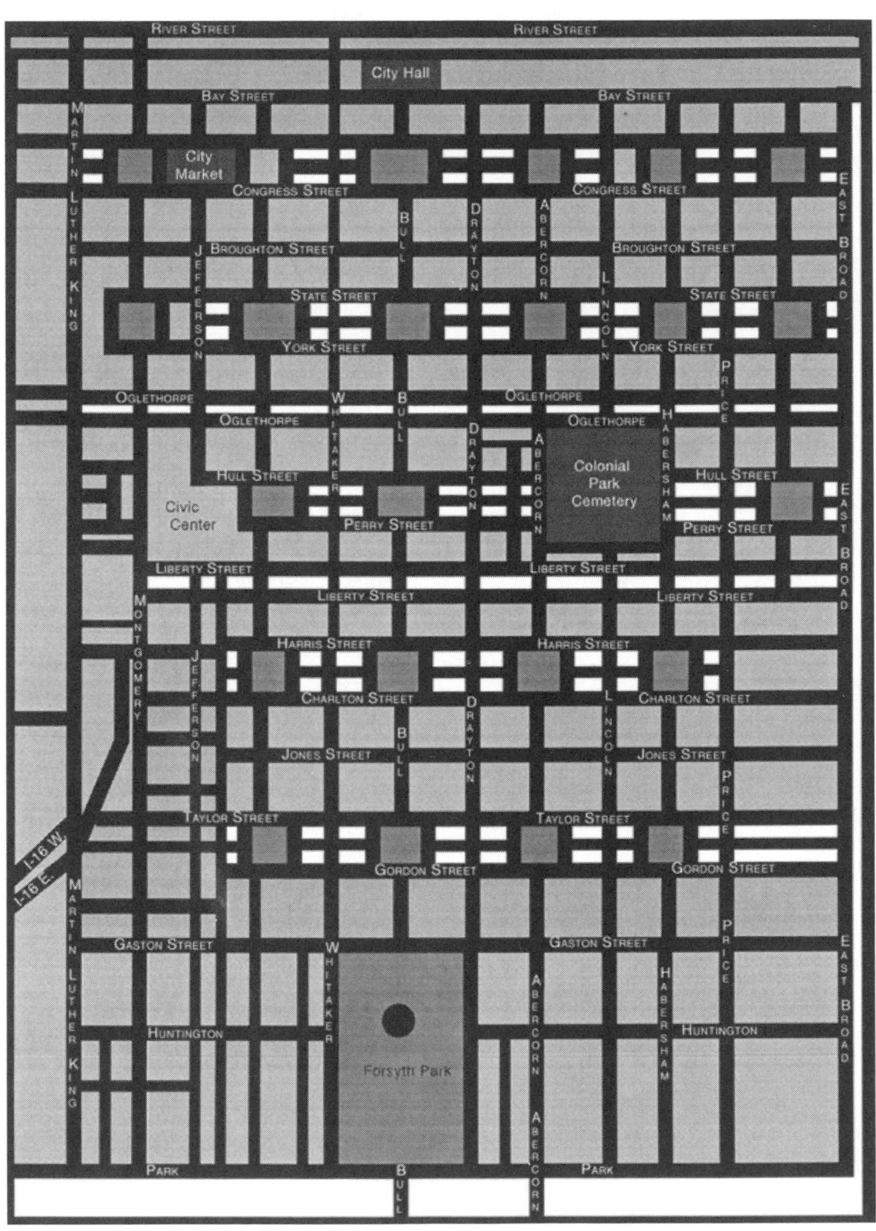


*Courtesy of Coastal Publishing, Inc. - Savannah*